Short Bike Rides™
in
Western Massachusetts

Second Edition

by
Howard Stone

An East Woods Book

The Globe Pequot Press

Old Saybrook, Connecticut

Cover design by Saralyn D'Amato-Twomey

Photograph on page 192 appears courtesy of the Massachusetts Department of Commerce and Development, Division of Tourism. All other photos appear courtesy of the author.

Library of Congress Cataloging-in-Publication Data

Stone, Howard.
    Short bike rides in western Massachusetts / by Howard Stone. — 2nd ed.
        p.   cm. — (Short bike rides series)
    "An East Woods book."
    Updated ed. of: Short bike rides in central and western Massachusetts. 1994
    Includes bibliographical references (p.   ).
    ISBN 0-7627-0076-9
    1. Bicycle touring—Massachusetts—Guidebooks. 2. Massachusetts—Guidebooks. I. Stone, Howard. Short bike rides in central and western Massachusetts. II. Title.   III. Series.
GV1045.5.M4S76 1997
796.6'4'09744—dc21   96-39641
                                                                                              CIP

Manufactured in the United States of America
Second Edition/First Printing

 This text and cover are printed on recycled paper.

Contents

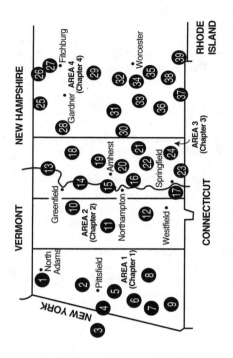

The numbers on this map refer to rides in this book.

Acknowledgments

This book could never have come to fruition without a lot of help. My wife, Bernice, provided continual encouragement, support, and late-night snacks. Dominique Coulombe, my supervisor, allowed me to work flexible hours so that I could take advantage of the daylight to research the rides. Jeanne LaFazia helped me interpret the intricacies of the laws of Massachusetts. Carla Petersen helped me type the manuscript. Andy Nosal, owner of The Map Center in Providence, told me about Hot Dog Annie's in Leicester. Dozens of local residents told me about hidden back roads and interesting places to see. I would also like to thank Kevin and Anita Clifford, Alan Moretsky, and Leesa Mann for putting me up overnight at various times.

Some of the photographs in the first edition were supplied by the Massachusetts Department of Commerce and Development, Division of Tourism. Mr. Leon White gave me full access to the photo collection and helped me choose scenes that would best capture the various landscapes of the state. In this edition I have used one of the photographs again.

Preface to the Second Edition

The second edition of *Short Bike Rides in Western Massachusetts* contains four new rides in the Berkshires and Taconic region and one new ride in the hill towns. The region east of Worcester and Fitchburg is covered in the companion volume *Short Bike Rides in Eastern Massachusetts*. The material follows the same format as the earlier work, with an introductory description, map, and point-to-point directions for each ride. The directions are somewhat more detailed to make them as easy to follow as possible.

Many of the rides have been modified slightly to improve scenery and safety, or to avoid badly deteriorated roads. Some of the starting points for rides in earlier editions now have parking "for customers only" or for short time periods. In these cases, I have changed the starting point to a location where parking is not a problem.

Introduction

This book is a guide to bicycling in Massachusetts west of Worcester and Fitchburg. The region, along with the sections of neighboring states just over the state line, offers ideal cycling. Massachusetts is blessed with an impressive network of thousands of back roads, most of them paved but not heavily traveled. Beyond the built-up metropolitan areas, which compose a very small percentage of the state, the landscape is rural enough to give the cyclist a sense of remoteness and serenity, and yet the nearest town, village, or grocery store is never more than a few miles away. The terrain is refreshingly varied for a relatively small state.

The Berkshires provide a perfect blend of scenic and cultural wealth—wooded mountains and soft green valleys dotted with lakes, estates, museums, and centers for the performing arts. The hill town region is the most rural part of the state, with rugged hills, deep valleys, and pristine small towns and villages. Central Massachusetts is an inspiring region of broad sweeps of farmland spreading along rugged hills and ridgetops, eventually sloping down to the broad valley of the Connecticut River.

Bicycling is an ideal way to appreciate the New England landscape's unique intimacy, which is not found in most other parts of the United States. The back roads turn constantly as they hug the minute contours of the land, forcing your orientation down to a small scale. Every turn and dip in the road may yield a surprise—a weathered barn, a pond, a stream, a little dam or falls, a hulking old mill right out of the Industrial Revolution, a ragged stone wall, or a pasture with grazing cattle or horses. Most of the smaller town centers are architectural gems, with the traditional stately white church and village green flanked by the town hall, a handsome brick or stone library, and graceful old wooden homes.

Geography of the Region

Western and central Massachusetts forms a rectangle that measures about 80 miles from east to west and about 50 miles from north to south. In general, the area is rolling or hilly except for the river valleys. As a result, biking in much of the region involves some effort. Most of the rides traverse at least one or two hills, sometimes steep or long enough that you'll want to walk them. To compensate, however, only a few hills are long enough to be really discouraging, and for every uphill climb there's a corresponding downhill run. The large majority of the hills you'll encounter are less than half a mile long, the steepest portion limited to a couple of hundred yards or less.

Culturally, Massachusetts has a long and proud history, beginning with the Pilgrim settlement in Plymouth in 1620. The first armed encounters of the Revolutionary War occurred a century and a half later in Concord and Lexington. The deep and sheltered harbors along the coast spawned thriving seaports, fisheries, and maritime commerce in Colonial times and into the nineteenth century. The Industrial Revolution got a head start in Massachusetts when Lowell and Holyoke, two of the first planned industrial cities in the country, evolved before the Civil War. In later years, culminating between the end of the Civil War and the turn of the century, hundreds of mills were built along the swift-flowing Housatonic, Westfield, Quaboag, and numerous other rivers, employing thousands of immigrants from Europe and French Canada.

Today hundreds of smaller towns and villages in Massachusetts make up some of the state's most appealing and architecturally fascinating hallmarks. As you bike through a town, try to notice each building along the green. First you'll see the graceful white church, usually built before 1850, often on a little rise, standing proudly above the rest of the town. Next look for the town hall, usually a handsome, white-pillared, Colonial-style building or an ornate wooden or stone Victorian one. Near the town hall you'll usually find the library, a gracious brick or stone building dating from the turn of the century or the two decades before it. The small-town library is almost always recognizable, generally built to appear dignified yet inviting, with wide steps, a portico framing the front door, and often a dome or rounded roof. Another building worth noticing is the schoolhouse. In the smaller towns, the schools are generally handsome old wooden or brick buildings, sometimes with graceful bell towers or cupolas.

Mill towns at first may look depressing, but there is always some architectural beauty to be found. The mills themselves are often fascinating old Victorian structures, forbidding but ornamented with cornices and clock towers. Next to the mill is usually a small millpond with a little dam or falls. Many mill towns have orderly rows of identical two- or three-story wooden houses, originally built for the workers during the late 1800s. Unfortunately, fire, neglect, and vandalism claim several mills each year, but a growing consciousness has arisen about preserving and maintaining these unique and impressive buildings. Many old mills have been recycled into apartments, condominiums, or offices.

Geographically, the region covered in this book is divided into four fairly distinct areas. The Berkshires, in Berkshire County at the western edge of the state, provide surprisingly enjoyable bicycling. Although this region contains the highest mountains in Massachusetts, most of the roads lie in the fertile valleys between them. In general, the grades tend to be long and steady rather than discouragingly steep. Most of the elevations are larger than hills but smaller than mountains, giving the region a gentle and intimate beauty rather than Colorado-like grandeur. Communities vary widely, from gracious college towns (Williamstown) to Victorian mill towns (North Adams, Adams, Lee) to elegant cultural centers (Lenox, Stockbridge) to numerous unspoiled villages. A unique feature of the Berkshires is its concentration of cultural attractions like museums, estates, former Shaker communities, music festivals, and centers for the performing arts, all in strikingly beautiful surroundings. Many writers, including Herman Melville, Nathaniel Hawthorne, and William Cullen Bryant came to the Berkshires in the mid-1800s, seeking peace and inspiration. Their lyrical descriptions of the region's beauty inspired industrialists, financial barons, and successful political figures to build summer mansions and estates (which they called "cottages") during the gilded age of the 1880s and 1890s, turning the Stockbridge-Lenox area into an inland Newport. In the 1930s three well-known performing arts festivals—the Tanglewood Music Festival, the Jacob's Pillow Dance Festival, and the Berkshire Theater Festival—transformed the Berkshires into a cultural mecca, and dozens more performing arts centers have become established in more recent years.

The area between the western edge of the Connecticut River Valley and Berkshire County comprises the hill towns. This region is the most undeveloped and sparsely populated portion of the state. It was also the last part of Massachusetts to be settled, because the steep slopes and rocky soil were unsuitable for farming and the rugged terrain made transportation difficult. Two-wheeled transportation is equally difficult—you can almost always count on a tough climb between towns. Most of the towns are lovely, with graceful white churches, attractive libraries, and inviting country stores. Scenic highlights of the region in-

3

clude the Bridge of Flowers in Shelburne Falls, a former trolley bridge that is now a pedestrian walkway lined with brilliant floral displays, and Chesterfield Gorge, a rockbound canyon carved by the Westfield River. The homestead of poet William Cullen Bryant in Cummington is the best-known historic site in the hill towns.

The Pioneer Valley, also called the Connecticut River Valley, provides the easiest bicycling in this book until you reach the hills at the valley's eastern edge. In the southern third of the state, the Connecticut River is heavily urbanized by Springfield, Chicopee, and Holyoke; but north of Holyoke it is delightfully rural as the broad, gracefully curving river winds between rich farms and tobacco fields, with the mountains rising dramatically at the edge of the valley several miles away. At the center of the region is a cluster of five colleges, three of them in Amherst. Ten miles south of the Vermont border is Old Deerfield, a restored community of elegant old homes. East of Amherst the landscape becomes very rural and very hilly—challenging but exciting to bicycle through. At the eastern edge of the region is the immense Quabbin Reservoir, by far the largest lake in the state. As in central Massachusetts, the towns in the Pioneer Valley are for the most part unspoiled gems. Some of the villages in the northern half of the state, such as New Salem, Wendell, and Warwick, seem unchanged from a hundred years ago except for cars in the driveways and pavement on the road.

Central Massachusetts covers the slice of state between Worcester and Fitchburg on the east and the Quabbin Reservoir on the west. This is one of the most rural and inspiringly beautiful parts of the state. The terrain is hilly and challenging for the cyclist, but the scenery more than makes up for it. The region is marked by an endless succession of hills and ridges, many crowned by broad, open farms that provide magnificent views. The Wachusett Reservoir, with its massive dam at the northern end in Clinton, is the second largest lake in the state. Almost without exception, the towns are graceful New England classics. The historic highlight of the region is Old Sturbridge Village, a superb reconstruction of a rural community from the early 1800s.

Massachusetts is fortunate to benefit from an active heritage of preserving its land and historic sites that began in the nineteenth century, before preservation was even considered in many other parts of the country. The state park system, run by the Department of Environmental Management, is admirable. A unique feature of the state park system is its responsibility for renovating old mills and factories, along with their adjacent waterways, into interpretive museums and visitor centers called Heritage State Parks. The names of two organizations, the Trustees of Reservations (TOR) and the Society for the Preservation of New England Antiquities (SPNEA), appear frequently in our descriptions of the rides. The first body is dedicated to acquiring and maintaining scenic areas, and it does the job admirably. TOR reservations are never shabby or shopworn, as so many other public areas are; instead, they are impeccably clean and well landscaped. Some of the finest natural areas in the state are TOR properties. The second body aims to acquire, preserve, and open to the public historic homes and mansions. Like TOR, it does a superb job. SPNEA properties, however, are open only during limited hours, usually afternoons in the summer. Largely a volunteer and member-supported organization, SPNEA simply does not have the funds to keep longer hours. In addition to these two bodies, dozens of other local historical societies and conservationist groups, including the Massachusetts Audubon Society, maintain historic houses and areas of greenspace.

One final geographic feature you'll encounter across the state is the drumlin, a small, sharp hill left behind by the glaciers. Most drumlins are elliptical like a football sliced lengthwise along the middle. They are usually less than a mile long and less than 200 feet high, and lie along a northwest–southeast or north–south axis, the direction of glacial flow. Clusters of drumlins are scattered across the state; one extensive drumlin region lies between Worcester and Springfield. In rural areas they transform the land into a rippling sea of rolling hills with broad pastures and orchards sweeping up and over them, providing some of the most inspiring and scenic bicycling in the state.

About the Rides

Ideally a bicycle ride should be a safe, scenic, relaxing, and an enjoyable experience that brings you into intimate contact with the landscape. In striving to achieve this goal, I've routed the rides along paved secondary and rural roads, avoiding main highways, larger cities, and dirt roads as much as possible. I've tried to make the routes as safe as possible. Hazards such as very bumpy roads or dead stops encountered while riding down a steep hill have been avoided whenever reasonable alternate routes exist. Dangerous spots are clearly indicated in the directions by a **CAUTION** warning. I've included scenic spots such as dams, falls, ponds, mill villages, or open vistas on the rides whenever possible.

Most of the rides have two options—a shorter one averaging about 15 miles long, and a longer one that is usually between 25 and 30 miles long. All the longer rides are extensions of the shorter ones, with both options usually starting off in the same way. A few rides, generally in remote areas, have no shorter option, and several have three alternatives. All the rides make a loop or figure-eight rather than backtracking along the same route. For each ride I include both a map and directions.

If you've never ridden any distance, the thought of riding 15 or, heaven forbid, 30 miles may sound intimidating or even impossible. I want to emphasize, however, that *anyone* in normal health can ride 30 miles and enjoy it if he or she gets *mildly* into shape first. You can accomplish this painlessly by riding at a leisurely pace for an hour several times a week for two or three weeks. At a moderate pace, you'll ride about 10 miles per hour. If you think of the rides by the hour rather than the mile, the numbers are much less frightening.

To emphasize how easy bicycle riding is, most bike clubs have a 100-mile ride, called a Century, each fall. Dozens of ordinary people try their first Century without ever having done much biking, and finish it, and enjoy it! Sure, they're tired at the end, but they've accomplished the feat and loved it. (If you'd like to try one, the biggest and flattest Century in the Northeast is held in southeastern Massachusetts on the Sunday after Labor Day—ask at any good bike shop for details.)

Not counting long stops, a 15-mile ride should take about two hours at a leisurely speed, a 20- to 25-mile ride about three hours, and a 30-mile ride about four hours. If you ride at a brisk pace, subtract an hour from these estimates.

A few of the rides in this book have short (half a mile or less) sections of dirt road. This was occasionally necessary when there was no simple alternate route, or to avoid making the directions needlessly complicated. If you come to a dirt road, get the feel of it first. If it's hard-packed, you can ride it without difficulty; but if it's soft, you should walk because it's easy to skid and fall unless you're on a mountain bike.

For every ride, I've recommended a starting point, but you can start anywhere else along the route if it's more convenient. For some of the rides between Worcester and Springfield you may want to start at the western edge of the ride if you're coming from the Springfield area, or at the eastern edge if you're coming from the Worcester area.

I have intentionally not listed the hours and fees of historic sites because they are subject to so much change, often from one year to the next. If it's a place you've heard of, it's probably open from 10 A.M. to 5 P.M., seven days a week. Unfortunately, many of the less frequently visited spots have limited hours—often only weekday afternoons during the summer, perhaps one day during the weekend. A few places of historic or architectural interest are open only by appointment because of funding and staffing considerations. Most historic sites are maintained by voluntary contributions and effort, and it's simply impossible to keep them staffed more than a few hours a day or a few months a year. If you really want to visit a site, call beforehand and find out the hours.

About the Maps

The maps are reasonably accurate but are not necessarily strictly to scale. Congested areas may be enlarged in relation to the rest of the map for the sake of legibility. All the maps adhere to these conventions:
1. Route numbers are circled.
2. Small arrows alongside the route indicate direction of travel.
3. The longer ride is marked by a heavy line. The shorter ride is marked by a dotted line where the route differs from that of the longer ride.
4. I've tried to show the angle of forks and intersections as accurately as possible.

Enjoying the Rides

You'll enjoy biking more if you add a few basic accessories to your bike and bring a few items with you.

1. **Handlebar bag with transparent map pocket on top.** It's always helpful to have some carrying capacity on your bike. Most handlebar bags are large enough to hold tools, a lunch, or even a light jacket. If you have a map or directions in your map pocket, it's much easier to follow the route. You simply glance down to your handlebar bag instead of fishing map or directions out of your pocket and stopping to read them safely. You may also wish to get a small saddlebag that fits under your seat or a metal rack that fits above the rear wheel, to carry whatever doesn't fit in the handlebar bag.

Always carry things on your bike, not on your back. A knapsack raises your center of gravity and makes you more unstable; it also digs painfully into your shoulders if you have more than a couple of pounds in it. It may do for a quick trip to the grocery store or campus, but never for an enjoyable ride when you'll be on the bike for more than a few minutes.

2. **Water bottle.** It is vital to carry water with you, especially in hot weather. On any ride of more than 15 miles, and any time the temperature is above 80 degrees, you will get thirsty, and if you don't drink enough water you will dehydrate. On longer rides through remote areas, or on a hot day, bring two or three water bottles. Put only water in your water bottles—it quenches thirst better than any other liquid.

3. **Basic tools.** Always carry a few basic tools with you when you go out for a ride, just in case you get a flat or a loose derailleur cable. Tire irons, a 6-inch adjustable wrench, a small pair of pliers, a small standard screwdriver, and a small Phillips-head screwdriver are all you need to take care of virtually all roadside emergencies. A rag and a tube of hand cleaner are useful if you have to touch your chain. If your bike has any Allen nuts (nuts with a small hexagonal socket on top), carry metric Allen wrenches to fit them. Cannondale makes a handy one-piece kit with four Allen wrenches, along with a standard and Phillips-head screwdriver.

4. **Pump and spare tube.** If you get a flat, you're immobilized unless you can pump up a new tube or patch the old one. Installing a brand new tube is less painful than trying to patch the old one on the road. Do the patching at home. Pump up the tire until it's hard, and you're on your way. Carry a spare tube in your handlebar bag, or wind it around the seat post, but make sure it doesn't rub against the rear tire.

If you bike a lot and don't use a mountain bike, you'll get flats—it's a fact of life. Most flats are on the rear wheel, because that's where most of your weight is. You should therefore practice taking the rear wheel off and putting it back on the bike, and taking the tire off and putting it on the rim, until you can do both confidently. It's much easier to practice at home than to fumble at it by the roadside.

5. **Dog repellent.** When you ride in rural areas you're going to encounter dogs, no two ways about it. Even if you don't have to use it, you'll have peace of mind knowing you have something like ammonia or commercial dog spray to repel an attacking dog if you have to. More on this later.

6. **Bicycle computer.** A bicycle computer provides a much more reliable way of following a route than depending on street signs or land-

marks. Street signs are often nonexistent in rural areas or are rotated 90 degrees by mischievous kids. Landmarks like "turn right at green house" or "turn left at Ted's Market" lose effectiveness when the green house is repainted red or Ted's Market goes out of business. Most computers indicate not only distance but also speed, elapsed time, and cadence (pedal strokes per minute). The solar-powered models last a long time before the batteries need replacement.

7. **Bike lock.** This is a necessity if you're going to leave your bike unattended. The best locks are the rigid, boltcutter-proof ones such as Kryptonite and Citadel. The next best choice is a strong chain or cable that can't be quickly severed by a normal-sized boltcutter or hacksaw. A cheap, flimsy chain can be cut in a few seconds and is not much better than no lock at all.

In urban or heavily touristed areas, always lock both wheels as well as the frame to a solid object and take your accessories with you when you leave the bicycle. Many a cyclist ignoring this simple precaution has returned to the vehicle only to find one or both wheels gone, along with the pump, water bottle, and carrying bags.

8. **Rear-view mirror.** A marvelous safety device, available at any bike shop, that enables you to check the situation behind you without turning your head. Once you start using a mirror, you'll feel defenseless without it. Most mirrors are designed to fit on either a bike helmet or the handlebars.

9. **Bike helmet.** Accidents happen, and a helmet will protect your head if you fall or crash. Bike helmets are light and comfortable, and more and more cyclists are using them.

10. **Food.** Always bring some food with you when you go for a ride. It's surprising how quickly you get hungry when you're biking. Some of the rides in this book go through remote areas with no food along the way, and that country store you were counting on may be closed on weekends or out of business. Fruit is nourishing and includes a lot of water. A couple of candy bars will provide a burst of energy for the last 10 miles if you're getting tired. (Don't eat candy or sweets before then—the energy burst lasts only about an hour, and then your blood-sugar level drops to below where it was before, and you'll be really weak.)

11. **Bicycling gloves.** Gloves designed for biking, with padded palms and no fingers, will cushion your hands and protect them if you fall. For maximum comfort, use handlebar padding also.

12. **Kickstand.** Using a kickstand is the most convenient way to

stand your bike upright without leaning it against a wall or other object. Keep in mind that a strong wind may knock your bike over and that in hot weather a kickstand may sink far enough into asphalt to topple your bike.

13. **Bike rack.** It is easier to use a bike rack than to wrestle your bike into and out of your car or trunk. Racks that attach to the back of the car are most convenient—do you really want to hoist your bike over your head onto the roof? If you use a rack that fits onto the back of the car, make sure that the bike is at least a foot off the ground and that the bicycle tire is well above the tailpipe. Hot exhaust blows out tires!

14. **Light.** Bring a bicycle light and reflective legbands with you in case you are caught in the dark. Ankle lights are lightweight and bob up and down as you pedal, giving additional visibility.

15. **Toilet paper.**

16. **Roll of electrical tape.** You never know when you'll need it.

If you are not concerned with riding fast, the most practical bicycle for recreational riding is either a mountain bike or a hybrid between a mountain bike and a sport bike. Most people find them more comfortable than sport bikes because the riding position is more upright. The gearing is almost always lower than it is on sport bikes, which makes climbing hills much easier. (If you buy a mountain bike, be sure to get one with 18 or 21 speeds.) Mountain bikes usually have thumb-operated shift levers, so you don't have to move your hands when shifting gears. The fatter, thicker tires are very resistant to punctures. Mountain bikes are very stable—you're less likely to skid or fall if you should go off the road into soft dirt or if you hit an obstacle like a sand patch, pothole, sewer grate, or bad bump. Mountain bikes are rugged and resistant to damage; for example, a pothole will often dent the rim of a sport bike but will not usually hurt a mountain bike. The only disadvantage of mountain bikes is that they are a little slower than other bicycles because of the wider tires and less streamlined riding position. If most of your riding is on pavement, you don't need standard mountain bike tires, which are about 2 inches wide with a deep, knobby tread. Use narrower tires (often called city tires or cross-training tires), which are $1\frac{3}{8}$ or $1\frac{1}{2}$ inches wide with a fairly smooth tread.

Take advantage of your gearing when you ride. It's surprising how many people with 21-speed bikes use only two or three of their gears. It takes less effort to spin your legs quickly in the low or middle gears than to grind along in the higher ones. For leisurely biking, a rate of about 80 revolutions per minute, or slightly more than one per second, is comfortable. If you find yourself grinding along at fewer than 70 RPMs, shift into a lower gear. Time your RPMs periodically on a watch with a second hand or your bicycle computer—keeping your cadence up is the best habit you can acquire for efficient cycling. You'll be less tired at the end of a ride and will avoid strain on your knees if you use the right gears.

If you have a 10- or 12-speed bike, you'll find it much easier to climb hills if you get a freewheel (the rear cluster of gears) that goes up to 34 teeth instead of the standard 28 teeth. You may also have to buy a new rear derailleur to accommodate the larger shifts, but the expense will be more than worthwhile in terms of ease of pedaling. For the ultimate in hill-climbing ease, you need an 18- or 21-speed bicycle. The smaller the inner front chainwheel, the lower the low gear. I recommend a small chainwheel with 24 or 26 teeth.

When approaching a hill, always shift into low gear *before* the hill, not after you start climbing it. If it's a steep or long hill, get into your lowest gear right away and go slowly to reduce the effort. Don't be afraid to walk up a really tough hill; it's not a contest, and you're out to enjoy yourself.

Here are few more hints to add to your cycling enjoyment: Adjust your seat to the proper height and make sure that it is level. Test for proper seat height by pedaling with your heels. Your leg should barely straighten out (with no bend) at the bottom of the downstroke. If your leg is bent, the seat is too low. If you rock from side to side as you pedal, the seat is too high.

Pedal with the balls of your feet, not your arches or heels, over the spindles. Toe clips are ideal for keeping your feet in the proper position on the pedals; they also give you added leverage when going uphill. The straps should be *loose* so that you can take your feet off the pedals effortlessly. In proper pedaling position, your leg should be slightly bent at the bottom of the downstroke.

Eat before you get hungry, drink before you get thirsty, and rest before you get tired. A good rule of thumb is to drink one water bottle per hour. To keep your pants out of your chain, tuck them inside your socks. Wear pants that are as seamless as possible. Jeans or cut-offs are the worst offenders; their thick seams are uncomfortable. For maximum comfort, wear padded cycling shorts or pants, with no underwear. Use a firm, good-quality seat. A soft, mushy seat may feel inviting, but as soon as you sit on it the padding compresses under your weight so that you're really sitting on a harsh metal shell.

If you have to use the bathroom, the simplest solution is to get out of sight off the road. A footpath or one-lane dirt road that curves out of sight into the woods is ideal. Most fast-food restaurants have easily accessible restrooms. If a restaurant is of the "Please wait to be seated" variety or has facilities "for customers only," either walk in briskly or order a snack. Most gas stations have restrooms; most convenience stores and country stores do not, but they will sometimes accommodate you if you ask urgently.

Using the Maps and Directions

Unfortunately, a book format does not lend itself to quick and easy consultation while you're on your bike. The rides will go more smoothly if you don't have to dismount at each intersection to consult the map or directions. You can solve this problem by making a photocopy of the directions and carrying it in your map pocket, dismounting occasionally to turn the sheet over or to switch sheets. Most people find it easier to follow the directions than the map.

In the directions, I have indicated the name of a road if there was a street sign at the time I researched the route; I designated the road as "unmarked" if the street sign was absent. Street signs have a short life span—a couple of years on the average—and are often nonexistent in rural areas. Very frequently, the name of a road changes without warning at a town line, crossroads, or other intersection.

Using a bicycle computer is virtually essential to enjoying the rides. The directions indicate the distance to the next turn or major intersection. Because so many of the roads are unmarked, you'll have to keep track accurately of the distance from one turn to the next. It is helpful to keep in mind that a tenth of a mile is 176 yards, or nearly twice the length of a football field.

In the written directions, it is obviously not practical to mention every single intersection. Always stay on the main road unless directed otherwise.

In addition to distances and a description of the next intersection, the directions also mention points of interest and situations that require caution. Any hazardous spot—for example, an unusually busy intersection or a bumpy section of road—has been clearly indicated by a **CAUTION** warning. It's a good idea to read over the entire tour before taking it in order to familiarize yourself with the terrain, points of interest, and places requiring caution.

In the directions certain words occur frequently, so let me define them to avoid any confusion.

To "bear" means to turn diagonally, somewhere between a 45-degree angle and going straight ahead. In these illustrations, you bear from road A onto road B.

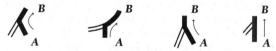

To "merge" means to come into a road diagonally, or even head-on, if a side road comes into a main road. In the examples, road A merges into road B.

A "sharp" turn is any turn sharper than 90 degrees; in other words, a hairpin turn or something approaching it. In the examples, it is a sharp turn from road A onto road B.

Safety

It is an unfortunate fact that thousands of bicycle accidents occur each year, with many fatalities. Almost all cycling accidents, however, are needless and preventable. Most accidents involve children under sixteen and are caused by foolhardy riding and failure to exercise common sense. The chances of having an accident can be reduced virtually to zero by having your bike in good mechanical condition, using two pieces of safety equipment (a rear-view mirror and a helmet), being aware of the most common biking hazards, and not riding at night unless prepared for it.

Before going out for a ride, be sure your bike is mechanically sound. Its condition is especially important if you bought the bike at a discount store, where it was probably assembled by a high school kid with no training. Above all, be sure that the wheels are secure and the brakes work.

Be certain your shoelaces are firmly tied, or use footwear with Velcro closures. A loose shoelace can wrap around the pedal axle or get caught in the chain, trapping you on the bicycle.

Invest in a rear-view mirror and a bicycle helmet, both available at any bike shop. Most mirrors attach to either your helmet or your handlebars and work as well as car mirrors when properly adjusted. The greatest benefit of having a mirror is that when you come to an obstacle such as a pothole or a patch of broken glass, you can tell at a glance whether or not it's safe to swing out into the road to avoid it. On narrow or winding roads you can always be aware of the traffic behind you and plan accordingly. Best of all, a mirror eliminates the need to peek back over your shoulder—an action that is not only awkward but also potentially dangerous, because you sometimes unconsciously veer toward the middle of the road while peeking.

A bicycle helmet is the cyclist's cheapest form of life insurance. A helmet not only protects your head if you land on it after a fall but also protects against the sun and the rain. More and more cyclists are wearing them, so you shouldn't feel afraid of looking odd if you use one. Helmets are light and comfortable; once you get used to one you'll never even know you have it on.

While on the road, use the same plain old common sense that you use while driving a car. Stop signs and traffic lights are there for a reason—obey them. At intersections, give cars the benefit of the doubt rather than trying to dash out in front of them or beat them through the light. Remember, they're bigger, heavier, and faster than you are. And you're out to enjoy yourself and get some exercise, not to be king of the road.

Several situations are inconsequential to the motorist but potentially hazardous for the bicyclist. When biking, try to keep aware of these:

1. **Road surface**. Not all roads in Massachusetts are silk-smooth. Often the bicyclist must contend with bumps, ruts, cracks, potholes, and

fish-scale sections of road that have been patched and repatched numerous times. When the road becomes rough, the only prudent course of action is to slow down and keep alert, especially going downhill. Riding into a deep pothole or wheel-swallowing crack can cause a nasty spill. On bumps, you can relieve some of the shock by getting up off the seat.

2. **Sand patches.** Patches of sand often build up at intersections, sharp curves, the bottoms of hills, and sudden dips in the road. Sand is very unstable if you're turning, so slow way down, stop pedaling, and keep in a straight line until you're beyond the sandy spot.

3. **Storm-sewer grates.** Federal regulations have outlawed thousands of hazardous substances and products, but unfortunately they have not yet outlawed the storm sewer with grates parallel to the roadway. This is a very serious hazard, because a cyclist catching the wheel in a slot will instantly fall, probably in a somersault over the handlebars. Storm sewers are relatively rare in rural areas but always a very real hazard.

4. **Dogs.** Unfortunately, man's best friend is the cyclist's worst enemy. When riding in the country you will encounter dogs, pure and simple. Even though many communities have leash laws, they are usually not enforced unless a dog really mangles someone or annoys its owners' neighbors enough that they complain—a rare situation because the neighbors probably all have dogs too.

The best defense against a vicious dog is to carry repellent—either ammonia in a squirtgun or plant sprayer (make sure it's leakproof), or a commercial dog spray called Halt, which comes in an aerosol can and is available at most bike shops. Repellent is effective only if you can grab it instantly when you need it—*don't* put it in your handlebar pack, a deep pocket, or anywhere else where you'll have to fish around for it. For Halt to work you have to squirt it directly into the dog's eyes, but if the dog is close enough to really threaten you, it's easily done.

The main danger from dogs is not being bitten, but rather bumping into them or instinctively veering toward the center of the road into oncoming traffic when the dog comes after you. Fortunately, almost all dogs have a sense of territory and will not chase you more than a tenth of a mile. If you're going along at a brisk pace and you're in front of the dog when it starts to chase you, you can probably outrun it and stay ahead until you reach the animal's territorial limit. If you're going at a leisurely pace, however, or heading uphill, or the dog is in the road in front of you, the only safe thing to do is dismount and walk slowly forward, keeping the bike between you and the dog, until you leave its territory. If the dog is truly menacing, or there's more than one, repellent can be comforting to have.

If you decide to stay on the bike when a dog chases you, always get into a low gear and spin your legs as quickly as possible. It's hard for a dog to bite a fast-rotating target. Many cyclists swing their pump at the animal, but this increases the danger of losing control of your bike. Often, yelling "Stay!" or "No!" in an authoritative voice will make a dog back off.

A word of caution about using commercial dog spray: It can be legally argued that dog spray comes under the Massachusetts firearms law, which carries a mandatory one-year jail sentence for carrying an unlicensed firearm. Such a case would probably not hold up in court, but because of the potential hazard, a zealous police officer might give you a hassle if he or she noticed it on your bike. The law states in Section 10 of Chapter 269, "Whoever . . . carries . . . a firearm . . . as defined in Section 121 of Chapter 140 . . . shall be punished by imprisonment. . . ." When you go to the definition in Section 121 of Chapter 140, it says, "Firearm shall mean a pistol, revolver or other weapon of any description loaded or unloaded, from which a shot or bullet can be discharged." A court would have to decide whether or not dog spray fits this definition.

5. **Undivided, shoulderless four-lane highways.** This is the most dangerous type of road for biking. If traffic is very light there is no problem, but in moderate or heavy traffic the road becomes a death trap unless you ride assertively. The only safe way to travel on such a road is to stay in or near the center of the right lane, rather than at the edge, forcing traffic coming up behind you to pass you in the left lane. If you hug the right-hand edge, some motorists will not get out of the right lane, brushing past you by inches or even forcing you off the road. Some drivers mentally register a bicycle as being only as wide as its tire, an unsettling image when the lane is not much wider than a car.

Several rides in this book contain short stretches along highways. If traffic is heavy enough to occupy both lanes most of the time, the only truly safe thing to do is walk your bike along the side of the road.

6. **Railroad tracks.** Tracks that cross the road at an oblique angle are a severe hazard, because you can easily catch your wheel in the slot between the rails and fall. NEVER ride diagonally across tracks—either walk your bike across or, if no traffic is in sight, cross the tracks at right

angles by swerving into the road. When riding across tracks, slow down and get up off the seat to relieve the shock of the bump.

7. **Oiled and sanded roads.** Many communities occasionally spread a film of oil or tar over the roads to seal cracks and then spread sand over the road to absorb the oil. The combination is treacherous for biking. Be very careful, especially going downhill. If the tar or oil is still wet, you should walk or you'll never get your bike clean.

8. **Car doors opening into your path.** This is a severe hazard in urban areas and in the center of towns. To be safe, any time you ride past a line of parked cars, stay 4 or 5 feet away from them. If oncoming traffic won't permit this, proceed very slowly and notice whether the driver's seat of each car is occupied. A car pulling to the side of the road in front of you is an obvious candidate for trouble.

9. **Low sun.** If you're riding directly into a low sun, traffic behind you may not see you, especially through a smeared or dirty windshield. Here your rear-view mirror becomes a lifesaver, because the only safe way to proceed is to glance constantly in the mirror and remain aware of conditions behind you. If you're riding directly away from a low sun, traffic coming toward you may not see you and could make a left turn into your path. If the sun is on your right or left, drivers on your side may not see you, and a car could pull out from a side road into your path. To be safe, give any traffic that may be blinded by the sun the benefit of the doubt, and dismount if necessary. Because most of the roads you'll be on are winding and wooded, you won't run into blinding sun frequently, but you should be aware of the problem.

10. **Kids on bikes.** Little kids riding their bikes in circles in the middle of the road and shooting in and out of driveways are a hazard; the risk of collision is always there because they aren't watching where they're going. Any time you see kids playing in the street, especially if they're on bikes, be prepared for anything and call out "Beep-beep" or "Watch out" as you approach. If you have a loud bell or horn, use it.

11. **Wet leaves.** In the fall, wet leaves are very slippery. Avoid turning on them.

12. **Metal-grate bridges.** When wet, the metal grating becomes very slippery, and you may be in danger of falling and injuring yourself on the sharp edges. If the road is wet, or early in the morning when there may be condensation on the bridge, please walk across.

A few additional safety reminders: If bicycling in a group, ride single file and at least 20 feet apart. Use hand signals when turning—to signal a right turn, stick out your right arm. If you stop to rest or examine your bike, get both your bicycle and yourself *completely* off the road. Sleek black bicycle clothing is stylish, but bright colors are safer and more visible.

Finally, use common courtesy toward motorists and pedestrians. Hostility toward bicyclists has received national media attention; it is caused by the 2 percent of discourteous cyclists (mainly messengers and groups hogging the road) who give the other 98 percent—responsible riders—a bad image. Please do not be part of the 2 percent!

Bikeways

There are currently only two bona fide bikeways, or bicycle paths, in the area covered by this book, although others are being planned. Both are in the Amherst–Northampton area. The Norwottuck Rail Trail, also called the Five-College Bike Path, runs for nearly 9 miles between the eastern edge of Northampton (at the Connecticut River) to Station Road in Amherst, following a course that is roughly parallel to Route 9. The other facility, the Northampton Bikeway, runs 2⁶/10 miles from Look Park to State Street north of the downtown area. There is a gap of about a mile between the two bikeways because an active railroad passes between them.

Bikeways are a mixed blessing. If well designed and well maintained, like the Cape Cod Rail Trail or the East Bay Bicycle Path in Rhode Island, they are a pleasure. If poorly designed or maintained, they are much more dangerous than the roads that they're supposed to avoid. Many bikeways are too narrow or have curves that are too sharp, and many have unsafe road crossings. Unless maintenance is vigilant, a bikeway will rapidly fill up with leaves, glass, and debris, and the surface will deteriorate. In good weather, all bikeways in populated areas will be used by pedestrians, joggers, rollerskaters, skateboarders, children, dogs, and other noncyclists.

The Bicycle Coalition of Massachusetts is actively striving to improve and increase bikeways. If you'd like to join in their efforts, contact them at 214A Broadway, Cambridge, MA 02139 (phone 617–491–RIDE).

Feedback

I'd be very grateful for any comments, criticisms, or suggestions about the rides in this book. Road conditions change, and a new snack bar or point of interest may open up along one of the routes. An intersection may be changed by road construction or improvement, or a traffic light may be installed. I'd like to keep the book updated by incorporating changes as they occur, or modifying a route if necessary in the interest of scenery or safety. Many of the changes I have made in previous editions have been inspired by riders' suggestions (for example, routing the Old Sturbridge Village Ride through the lovely town center of Warren). Please feel free to contact me through the Globe Pequot Press, P.O. Box 833, Old Saybrook, CT 06475-0833 with any revision you think helpful.

Chapter 1:
The Berkshires

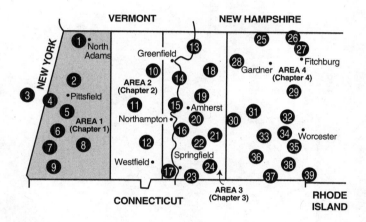

The numbers on this map refer to rides in this book.

Church in Adams

The Northwest Corner:
North Adams–Williamstown–Adams

Number of miles: 26 (15 without Adams extension)
Terrain: Gently rolling, with several moderate hills.
Food: Restaurants and grocery stores in the towns. Restaurant next to starting point.
Start: Western Gateway Heritage State Park, Furnace Street, North Adams. It's ³/₁₀ mile south of Route 2 and immediately west of Route 8.
How to get there: From Route 2 get onto Route 8 South (you have to make three turns if you're coming from the east on Route 2). Go ³/₁₀ mile to Furnace Street on right, at far end of overpass. Turn right, and immediately bear right to park. From Pittsfield follow Route 8 into North Adams. Turn left on Furnace Street immediately before overpass (it's just before the center of town), and bear right into park.

The northwest corner of Massachusetts is a fascinating area with three towns of widely contrasting character. Adams and North Adams are well-preserved mill towns brimming with Victorian architecture, while Williamstown is the epitome of the gracious New England college town. All three towns lie at the base of mighty Mount Greylock, which at nearly 3,500 feet is the highest mountain in the state. Dramatic views of the mountain greet you around almost every bend. Although the area is mountainous, the ride is one of the easiest in the Berkshires because all the roads are in the valley of the Hoosic River. (If you really want to bike up Greylock, you may; the route is in Lewis Cuyler's book, *Bike Rides in the Berkshire Hills.*)

North Adams, where the ride starts, is a town of striking visual impact. The downtown area contains two blocks of handsome five- and six-story commercial buildings from the late 1800s. Next to the center of town are a cluster of four magnificent churches with tall spires, the turreted public library, and ornate Victorian houses. Along the river lie massive Dickensian mills and rows of duplex and triplex mill houses. The hillside behind the starting point provides a fine view of the town, its church steeples outlined against the mountains to the east.

The starting point, Western Gateway Heritage State Park, is a museum devoted primarily to the building of the Hoosac Tunnel between 1851 and 1875. The railroad tunnel, blasted through nearly 5 miles of solid rock, provided a direct route between Boston and the Great Lakes, and ultimately, the developing West. The state park is housed in a complex of former railroad buildings that now contains shops and restaurants as well as museum exhibits.

From North Adams you'll head west to Williamstown on Route 2. Although busy, the road is wide enough to be safe for bicycling. After about 2 miles you'll go through the village of Greylock (part of North Adams), dominated by a large brick mill. As you arrive in Williamstown, you'll loop south through a gracious residential area before passing through the center of town and the lovely campus of Williams College. Shortly before the campus the route passes the Sterling and Francine Clark Art Institute, one of two superb art museums in Williamstown. It has a strong collection of French impressionist paintings. About a mile ahead is the Williams College Museum of Art, which emphasizes American and contemporary art. Also on the campus (which is perfectly integrated into the town) are two large, stately churches and the handsome Williamstown Memorial Library.

The ride returns to North Adams via a secondary road that runs parallel with Route 2 along the north bank of the Hoosic River. As you arrive in town you'll see a huge brick mill complex; there are plans to turn it into a museum of contemporary art.

The long ride heads south from North Adams for about 5 miles to Adams. This portion of the ride, which follows the eastern edge of the Hoosic River Valley, provides stunning views of Mount Greylock, which towers 2,500 feet above the valley floor. The flatiron-shaped scar just below the summit was caused by a landslide in 1990 after heavy rains. Like North Adams, Adams has fine brick business buildings in the downtown area, several impressive churches, and an attractive library built in 1897. (The ride does not go through the center of town but comes within a few blocks of it.) As you leave Adams you'll ride past several long, brick rowhouses reminiscent of a Welsh mining town and see limestone quarries etched into the base of the mountainside. You'll return to the starting point along Route 8, a table-flat road with good shoulders.

Directions for the rides ～～～～～～～～～～～～

1. Follow Furnace Street to Route 8. Turn left (north) and go less than $4/10$ mile to second traffic light (sign points right to Routes 2 and 8 North).

2. Turn right at second light and go $1/10$ mile to end.

3. Turn right at end and immediately turn right again on Route 2 West at traffic light. Go $4^8/10$ miles to Route 43 (Water Street) on left, in Williamstown. It's just after a traffic light where Cole Avenue turns right.

4. Turn left on Route 43 and go $1^1/10$ miles to Gale Road on right, shortly after Ide Road on right.

5. Turn right on Gale Road and go $1^7/10$ miles to Route 2 East on right, immediately after stop sign.

The Clark Art Institute will be on your left after $1^2/10$ miles, at the top of a short hill. When you get to Route 2 East, there's a small park on the left. In the center of the park stands the 1753 House, a replica of a small dwelling constructed by Williamstown's orignal settlers. The reproduction was built in 1953 by volunteers as part of the town's bicentennial celebration.

6. Turn right on Route 2 East and go $6/10$ mile to Cole Avenue on left, at traffic light.

You'll pass through the campus of Williams College; most of it is on the left. Spring Street, the town's main shopping street, is on the right after $3/10$ mile. The Williams College Museum of Art is on the right just ahead, immediately before you start to go downhill (it's in Lawrence Hall, set back a short distance from the road). The small, stone, turreted building on the right midway down the hill is a planetarium.

7. Turn left on Cole Avenue and go $8/10$ mile to end. You'll pass a handsome brick church on the left and then an old brick mill on the right just before the end.

8. Turn right at end and go 3 miles to fork. You'll have good views of Mount Greylock on the right. After about 2 miles you'll ride through the village of Blackinton (part of North Adams), where you'll pass a brick mill and a small stone church on the right and, just ahead, a Gothic-style church built in 1871 on the left.

9. Bear left at fork and go $1^1/2$ miles to traffic light (Houghton Street on left, Marshall Street on right). The massive mill complex on the right just before the intersection is the proposed location for the Massachusetts Museum of Contemporary Art.

10. Turn right on Marshall Street and go ²⁄₁₀ mile to second traffic light (Main Street). Here the long ride turns left, but if you're doing the short ride continue straight for ¼ mile to Furnace Street on right, at far end of overpass. Turn right on Furnace Street, and the starting point is just ahead on the right.

11. Turn left on Main Street into downtown North Adams. Go ²⁄₁₀ mile to fork where Church Street bears right, at top of short hill. Three fine churches cluster around the intersection. The ornate, Victorian building on the far right corner is the public library.

12. Bear right on Church Street and go 1³⁄₁₀ miles to stop sign (merge left on Route 8A). **CAUTION:** Watch for potholes near end. You'll pass North Adams State College on the right after ⁶⁄₁₀ mile.

13. Bear left on Route 8A and go 1¹⁄₁₀ miles to Church Street on left, just before a large school on left. Route 8A curves sharply right at the intersection.

14. Turn left on Church Street and go 2⁹⁄₁₀ miles to crossroads (East Hoosac Street), at the bottom of a little hill. You'll enjoy spectacular views of Mount Greylock on the right.

15. Turn right on East Hoosac Street and go ½ mile to crossroads and stop sign (Summer Street), in Adams. A magnificent brick church guards the far left corner. Here the ride turns right, but if you'd like to see the center of town, go straight for ³⁄₁₀ mile to end (Route 8), turn left, and go ²⁄₁₀ mile.

16. Turn right on Summer Street and go less than ⁴⁄₁₀ mile to second crossroads (Kittler Avenue).

17. Turn left on Kittler Avenue and go ¹⁄₁₀ mile to end (Crotteau Street).

18. At end, jog right and immediately left on Cook Street. Go ¹⁄₁₀ mile to end (Route 8).

19. Turn right on Route 8 and go 4⁶⁄₁₀ miles to Furnace Street on left, immediately before overpass. **CAUTION:** Dangerous diagonal railroad tracks after ¾ mile. You'll pass several long, brick rowhouses on your left at the beginning.

20. Turn left on Furnace Street. The starting point is just ahead on the right.

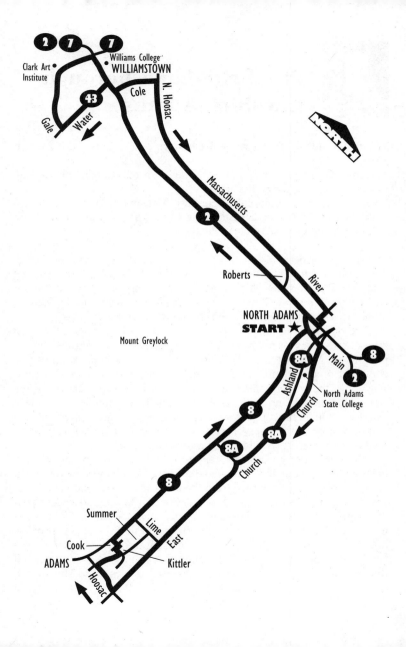

2 Pittsfield–Lanesborough–Cheshire–Adams

Number of miles: 30 (15 without Cheshire–Adams extension, 25 with shortcut omitting Adams)
Terrain: The short ride is gently rolling with one tough hill and one moderate one. The long rides are hilly.
Food: Grocery and restaurant in Cheshire. McDonald's at end.
Start: McDonald's, Allendale Shopping Center, at the junction of Route 9, Route 8, and Crane Avenue in Pittsfield.

The region northeast of Pittsfield, heading toward Adams, is very pleasant for bicycling. The dominant features of the landscape are the Cheshire Reservoir, which is nearly 4 miles long, and views of Mount Greylock to the north. Pittsfield thins out quickly as you head north out of the city, and the secondary roads have very little traffic.

The ride starts in the northeastern part of Pittsfield from a shopping center that strives for uniqueness by planting half a boat vertically in the parking lot. Within a mile the landscape starts to become rural as you climb out of a residential area. A beautiful back road traverses the hillside above the western shore of the Cheshire Reservoir (also called the Hoosac Reservoir), and then descends gradually to Route 8 just south of Cheshire. You'll return to the starting point on Route 8, which hugs the opposite shore of the reservoir closely for the first couple of miles. This road is moderately traveled and has a good shoulder.

The long rides go into the center of Cheshire, an attractive small town with a traditional New England church and a handsome town hall built in 1898. Across the road from the post office is a monument in the shape of a cheese press. It commemorates a 1,235-pound cheese produced in 1801 from local dairy farms and sent to President Thomas Jefferson in Washington. A long climb brings you into the hills east of the town, where you'll see Mount Greylock rising in dramatic splendor beyond the fields of grazing cows. If you wish, you may go about a mile off the route to visit another unusual memorial, the Stafford Hill Monument. It is a circular stone structure with graceful arches built in 1927; a Revolutionary War hero is buried here. Behind the monument is an inspiring view of Mount Greylock.

As you approach Adams, you'll ride along an open ridge with magnificent views before plunging steeply downhill into the outskirts of town. The downtown area (just off the route) contains attractive brick commercial buildings from the late nineteenth century, several impressive churches, and a handsome library built in 1897. From Adams the route ascends once again into the hills south of town, loops downhill back into Cheshire, and rejoins the short ride.

Directions for the rides ~~~~~~~~~~~~~~~~

1. Turn right out of the south end of the parking lot, with McDonald's on your left as you leave the lot. Immediately bear right at stop sign on Crane Avenue (unmarked). Go $^4/_{10}$ mile to Oak Hill Road on right.

2. Turn right on Oak Hill Road and go $2^8/_{10}$ miles to end. After about a mile you'll climb steeply for $^3/_{10}$ mile. This is the worst hill of the short ride. Then you'll see Berkshire Mall on the right and Mount Greylock straight ahead. Oak Hill Road becomes Partridge Road.

3. Turn left at end and go $^4/_{10}$ mile to Cheshire Road on right.

4. Turn right on Cheshire Road and go $4^2/_{10}$ miles to end (Route 8). You'll ride through rolling farmland, with glimpses of the Cheshire Reservoir nestled below on the right. The 30- and 25-mile rides turn left on Route 8; for the 15-mile ride, turn right on Route 8 and go $6^7/_{10}$ miles to shopping center on right. You'll follow the shore of the Cheshire Reservoir for the first $2^1/_2$ miles.

5. Turn left on Route 8 and go $^3/_{10}$ mile to traffic light, in Cheshire. There's a graceful white church on the far right corner.

6. Turn right at traffic light and go $^1/_2$ mile to fork immediately after metal-grate bridge. **CAUTION** crossing bridge; walk across if the road is wet.

7. Go straight ahead at fork (don't bear left). Go $^6/_{10}$ mile to another fork where Notch Road bears right and Windsor Road bears left. **CAUTION:** There's another metal-grate bridge after $^2/_{10}$ mile. It's a steep climb from the bridge to the fork.

8. Bear left on Windsor Road and go $2^2/_{10}$ miles to crossroads where Richmond Hill Road turns right and Stafford Hill Road turns left. Most of this stretch is uphill, with two very steep pitches. There are fine views of

Mount Greylock on your left.

At the crossroads the ride goes straight, but if you'd like to visit the Stafford Hill Monument, turn left. Go $\frac{9}{10}$ mile to a one-lane dirt road on the left, immediately after a blue-gray house on the left with a long driveway. Follow the one-lane road $\frac{1}{10}$ mile to the monument. Stafford Hill Road climbs steeply for $\frac{3}{10}$ mile; then it levels off and becomes dirt. The view from the monument is partially obscured by trees; there's a better view from the field behind it.

9. Go straight at crossroads (left if you visited the monument) for $2\frac{2}{10}$ miles to end (merge left on Route 116; there is no stop sign). **CAUTION:** Bumpy spots near the beginning, while going downhill. Mount Greylock looms in front of you near the end.

Here the ride turns sharply right, but if you'd like to shorten the ride by 5 miles (the 25-mile ride), bear left on Route 116 and go $\frac{1}{10}$ mile to Wells Road on left. Resume with direction number 14, turning left on Wells Road instead of right.

10. Turn sharply right on Route 116 and go $\frac{1}{10}$ mile to Henry Wood Road on left.

11. Turn left on Henry Wood Road and go $2\frac{1}{10}$ miles to East Street on left.

At the beginning you'll ascend with wonderful views in all directions, including behind you. Immediately before the intersection you'll see an old white house on the right. Susan B. Anthony, a leader of the women's suffrage movement, was born here in 1820.

12. Turn left on East Street and go $\frac{9}{10}$ mile to end (Route 116). **CAUTION:** Curving, very steep descent—take it easy. Here the ride turns left, but if you'd like to visit the center of Adams, turn right and proceed $\frac{3}{10}$ mile.

13. Turn left on Route 116 South, heading uphill. Go $2\frac{1}{10}$ miles to Wells Road on right, shortly after high school on left. You'll climb steeply for the first $\frac{6}{10}$ mile.

14. Turn right on Wells Road (don't go onto the dirt road) and go $3\frac{8}{10}$ miles to traffic light (Route 8), back in Cheshire. **CAUTION:** After $3\frac{3}{10}$ miles you'll cross the metal-grate bridge again.

Most of this section is downhill, with good views of Mount Greylock on the right. The Cheese Press Monument is on the right just after the bridge, across from the post office.

15. Turn left on Route 8 and go 7 miles to shopping center on right. You'll follow the shore of the Cheshire Reservoir, on your right, to the beginning.

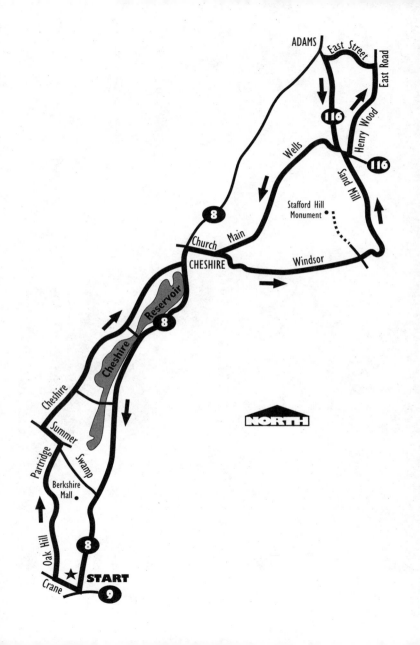

Chatham, New York

Chatham, New York

Number of miles: 21

Terrain: Mostly gently rolling, with one steady climb a mile long and several short hills.

Food: Country store and restaurant in Old Chatham. Restaurant in Chatham, at end.

Start: Old train station on Route 66 in Chatham, immediately south of Route 295. Park where legal on Route 66.

How to get there: Chatham is about 30 miles southeast of Albany, 1½ miles west of the Taconic State Parkway near its northern end, and midway between the Hudson River and the Massachusetts border. From the Parkway take the Route 203 exit, which is 5 miles south of the Berkshire extension of the New York State Thruway (I–90). Turn right on Route 203 if you're coming from the south and left if you're coming from the north. Go about 1½ miles to Route 66, at traffic light. Turn right (north) on Route 66 and go ³⁄₁₀ mile to train station on left. Park across from the station on the block immediately before it (there are time restrictions on the next block) or in front of the station on the southbound side of Route 66.

The Chatham region, about 5 to 10 miles west of the Massachusetts border and 25 miles southeast of Albany, provides superb bicycling past prosperous farms and rolling hillsides. Back roads with very little traffic curl past old barns and soft green meadows where horses and cattle graze. The wonderful Shaker Museum, which you'll visit about halfway through the ride, is a historical highlight.

The ride starts from the center of Chatham, an attractive small town with a brick business block dating from the late nineteenth century, a dignified town hall with pillars framing the doorway, and a weathered old train station that was built in 1877. You'll promptly head into rural countryside, where Route 66 rolls past perfectly groomed horse and dairy farms with hills rising in the distance—the predominant landscape of the ride. After a few miles you'll descend into Chatham Center, a hamlet with a few houses and a graceful white church. From here you'll pedal through the fertile valley of Kinderhook Creek to the hamlet of Malden Bridge, where you'll pass an art gallery, two antiques shops, and a handsome brick house.

An idyllic country lane leads about 2 miles from Malden Bridge to the Shaker Museum. The Shakers, who flourished during the middle of the nineteenth century, are the best known and among the most fascinating of America's communal sects. Their belief in celibacy ensured their eventual demise. Their lifestyle was strictly regimented and spartan, but not to the point of privation or misery. Shaker architecture, artifacts, and furnishings are unique because they combine form and function with almost spiritual simplicity. The museum, which contains several rustic buildings surrounded by fields and horse farms, provides a wonderful opportunity to gain an understanding of the Shaker way of life. In addition to furniture and household implements, the museum also displays a blacksmith shop, a weaving studio, and a schoolroom. Other exhibits pertain to the Shakers' agriculture and medicinal herb industry.

The gracious hamlet of Old Chatham, where an inviting country store and several fine houses cluster around the main intersection, is shortly after the Shaker Museum. You may wish to grab a snack here to boost you up the mile-long hill just ahead. But you'll be rewarded by a steep drop into East Chatham and then a gradual descent for several miles back to Chatham.

Directions for the ride

1. Head north on Route 66. You will immediately come to a fork where Route 295 bears right and Route 66 bears left.
2. Bear left on Route 66. **CAUTION:** Walk your bike through this dangerous intersection, which has railroad tracks running diagonally through it. Go less than ²⁄₁₀ mile to a small traffic circle at the far end of the business district.

Notice the brick-pillared town hall on your right at the traffic circle.
3. Go three quarters of the way around the traffic circle, staying on Route 66 North (**CAUTION** here). Go 4⁴⁄₁₀ miles to fork where County Road 17 goes straight and Route 66 bears right.

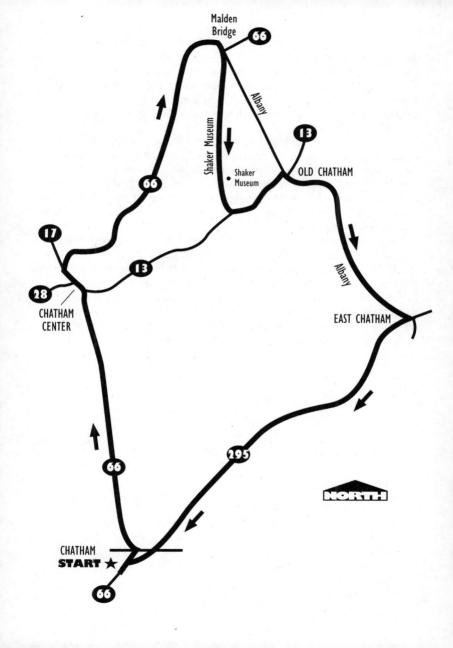

The road rolls past horse farms and grassy hillsides. You'll ride through the hamlet of Chatham Center ½ mile before the fork. Notice the stately white church, with pillars framing the entrance, on your right.

4. Bear right on Route 66 and go 4⁴/10 miles to the intersection where Route 66 turns left, just after a bridge. The hamlet of Malden Bridge, with a handsome brick house on your left and a couple of antiques shops, is just before the bridge.

5. Go straight and immediately bear right on Shaker Museum Road (un-marked), passing a small church on your left. Notice the bell in front of the church. Go 2⁶/10 miles to end (County Road 13). You'll ride past tidy horse farms and come to the Shaker Museum on your left after 2¹/10 miles.

6. Turn left on County Road 13 and go 1 mile to end, at top of hill, in the village of Old Chatham. There's a country store on your right at the inter-section and a restaurant across the road.

7. Turn right at end. Go 3¹/10 miles to crossroads and stop sign immedi-ately after railroad bridge (Route 295) in East Chatham.

At the beginning there's a steady climb a mile long, but once you're at the top, the rest of the ride is mostly downhill. The road parallels the Berkshire extension of the New York State Thruway on your right.

8. Turn right on Route 295 (it's a fairly sharp right). Go 5³/10 miles to end, at stop sign (merge left on Route 66). This section is mostly wooded.

9. Bear left on Route 66. The train station is immediately ahead on your right.

4 The Shaker Village Ride:
Pittsfield–Richmond–Canaan, New York–
New Lebanon, New York

Number of miles: 26 (14 without Canaan–New Lebanon extension)
Terrain: The short ride is rolling. The long ride is hilly, with a steep, 2½-
mile climb toward the end.
Food: Apple and cider store in Richmond. Convenience store and country store in Canaan. Restaurant in New Lebanon.
Start: McDonald's on Route 20 (West Housatonic Street) in Pittsfield,
1¹⁄₁₀ miles west of Route 7. If the parking lot is designated "Customers
Only" or parking is limited to a short period of time, start from the shopping center across the street.

The area west and a little south of Pittsfield, straddling the Massachusetts–
New York border, provides scenic bicycling past farms with hills and
mountains rising in the distance. The rugged Taconic Range, which
you'll struggle across on the longer ride, runs along the state line and extends a short distance westward into New York. A historic highlight of
the ride are two former Shaker communities—Mount Lebanon Shaker
Village, which you'll see on the long ride, and Hancock Shaker Village,
which is on the route of both rides.

The ride starts from the west side of Pittsfield, and within a mile you'll
leave the built-up part of the city behind. Fortunately for the bicyclist,
Pittsfield is a compact city unmarred by urban sprawl. Richmond, the
town bordering Pittsfield on the southwest, has a population of less than
2,000; Hancock, which is squeezed between the city and the New York
state line, has fewer than 1,000 residents. You'll follow a secondary road
southwest into Richmond, passing small farms and an apple orchard. As
you approach the state line, the landscape becomes more rolling, with
steep little ups and downs that are fun to bicycle over if you use your
gears properly. Just before the state line, the route turns north along
quiet side roads to Route 20, which will bring you back to Pittsfield.

You'll arrive at Hancock Shaker Village just after you turn east onto
Route 20. The Shakers, who flourished during the middle of the nine-

teenth century, are the best known of America's communal sects (see ride 3 for more detail). The Shaker Village, which contains twenty original buildings surrounded by broad expanses of farmland, provides a wonderful opportunity to gain an understanding of the Shaker way of life. The most distinctive building is a round stone barn about 85 feet in diameter; it was designed to allow one person standing in the center to feed an entire herd of cattle.

From the Shaker Village it's about 3½ miles back to the starting point along Route 20. The road is moderately traveled, gently rolling, and fairly wide.

The long ride heads farther west across the state line into Canaan, New York. You'll pass through a gap in the Taconic Range, with a short hill followed by a long, steady descent into a valley just west of the border. A back road hugs the shore of Queechy Lake. Then you'll ride gradually downhill through the valley into the village of New Lebanon, which is bordered by beautiful rolling farmland.

East of New Lebanon there is no gap in the Taconic Range, so you'll have to endure a steady, 2½-mile climb to get across it. After about a mile you can take a break by visiting Mount Lebanon Shaker Village, which is much less visited than the one in Hancock. Mount Lebanon, which also contains about twenty handsome brick and wooden buildings, served as the spiritual center for the entire Shaker movement (analogous to the Vatican for the Catholic Church) between 1820 and 1860. Some of the buildings form the campus of the Darrow School, a small preparatory school. The stone barn was the largest of its kind in North America when it was built in 1851 (it was destroyed by fire in 1972, but the shell remains standing). A small Sufi community, called Abode of the Message, is located beyond the school. The Sufis are Islamic mystics; their ultimate goal is union with God.

The climb continues for nearly 2 miles beyond Mount Lebanon, with a magnificent view just before the top. Then it's all downhill to Hancock Shaker Village, just before which you'll rejoin the short ride.

Directions for the ride: 26 miles ～～～～～～～

1. Turn right on Route 20 (left if you're starting from the shopping center) and go ¼ mile to Barker Road on right, immediately after blinking traffic light.

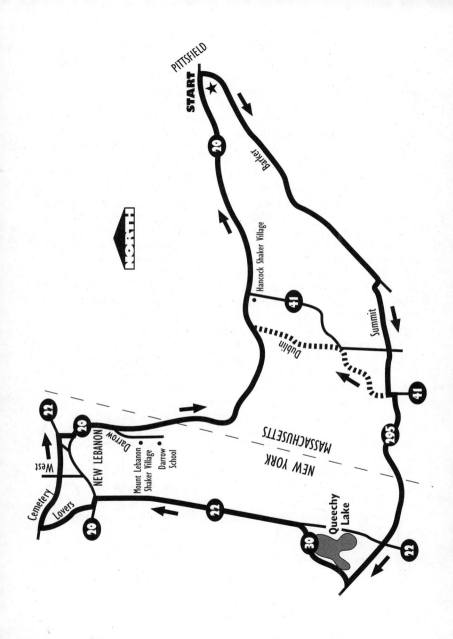

2. Turn right on Barker Road and go $4\frac{1}{2}$ miles to Summit Road on right, at top of short hill. Lenox Mountain dominates the landscape ahead of you toward the left. You'll pass Bartlett's Orchard, an excellent apple and cider store, on the left shortly before the intersection.

3. Turn right on Summit Road and go 2 miles to end (Route 41). Here the short ride turns right, and the long ride turns left. Summit Road is very rolling, with short, steep ups and downs.

4. Turn left on Route 41 and go $\frac{1}{10}$ mile to Route 295 (Canaan Road) on right.

5. Turn right on Route 295 and go $2\frac{4}{10}$ miles to traffic light (Route 22). There's a short hill at the beginning and a long, relaxing descent at the end. You'll enter New York State $\frac{8}{10}$ mile before the intersection. When you get to Route 22 there's a grocery on the left, but you'll come to a more appealing country store a mile up the road.

6. Cross Route 22 and go $\frac{9}{10}$ mile to Columbia County Route 30, which turns sharply right (the route sign is visible after you make the turn). The Canaan Market is on your right at the intersection.

7. Turn sharply right on Route 30 and go $1\frac{4}{10}$ miles to end (Route 22 again). This is a beautiful ride along Queechy Lake. When you come to Route 22, the Berkshire Farm Center, a rehabilitation center for nonviolent juvenile offenders, is on the far side of the intersection.

8. Turn left on Route 22 and go $3\frac{4}{10}$ miles to end (Route 20), in New Lebanon. Most of this section is a gradual descent through a valley, with the Taconic Range rising sharply on both sides of the road. There's an attractive fieldstone church on your left at the end.

9. Turn left on Route 20 and go $\frac{1}{10}$ mile to Lovers Lane on right. The Sandpiper Family Restaurant, on your left at the intersection, is a good spot for a bite.

10. Turn right on Lovers Lane and go $\frac{8}{10}$ mile to end (Cemetery Road, unmarked).

11. Turn right at end and go $\frac{8}{10}$ mile to crossroads and stop sign (West Street, Columbia County Route 5A). You'll enjoy views of rolling fields with mountains in the background.

12. Continue straight for $\frac{4}{10}$ mile to stop sign (merge head-on onto Route 22).

13. Go straight on Route 22 for less than $\frac{2}{10}$ mile to unmarked road on the right (sign may say TO ROUTE 20 EAST). Notice the handsome stucco school on the left immediately before the intersection and the graceful stone church on the right just past the intersection.

14. Turn right on this road and go ³/₁₀ mile to end (Route 20). At the end, look to your right for a great view.

15. Turn left on Route 20, beginning the long climb over the Taconic Range. Go ⁸/₁₀ mile to Darrow Road on right.

16. Turn right on Darrow Road, go ¼ mile to Mount Lebanon Shaker Village, and backtrack to Route 20. The stone shell of the massive barn, destroyed by fire in 1972, is on the right. The handsome wood and brick buildings of the Darrow School, originally part of the Shaker community, are ²/₁₀ mile beyond the Shaker Village. The Abode of the Message (the Sufi community) is shortly after the school.

17. Turn right on Route 20 and go 4 miles to the Hancock Shaker Village on right. You'll ascend ⁸/₁₀ mile to the Massachusetts state line and continue uphill another mile to the summit. Just before the top, an overlook on the right provides a panoramic view. Then it's all downhill to the Shaker Village.

18. Continue on Route 20 for 3⁴/₁₀ miles to McDonald's on right.

Directions for the ride: 14 miles ～～～～～～～

1. Follow directions for the long ride through number 3.

2. Turn right on Route 41 and go 1²/₁₀ miles to crossroad (Dublin Road). You'll pass an old cemetery on the right after ¼ mile.

3. Turn left on Dublin Road and go 1⁶/₁₀ miles to end (Route 20).

4. Turn right on Route 20 and go 3⁹/₁₀ miles to McDonald's on right. Hancock Shaker Village will be on your right after ½ mile.

Lenox Loop:
Pittsfield–Lenox–Richmond

Number of miles: 25 (15 without Lenoxdale–Richmond extension)
Terrain: The short ride is rolling; the long ride is hilly.
Food: Grocery and restaurants in Lenox. Store selling apples and cider in Richmond.
Start: Corner of South Street (Routes 7 and 20) and Taylor Street, in Pittsfield. It's ⁷/₁₀ mile south of the center of the city and ½ mile south of Route 20 West. Park on Taylor Street facing South Street.

CAUTION:

The long ride goes past Tanglewood, which breeds traffic jams on the narrow nearby roads before and after concerts. The concert season runs from the beginning of July through Labor Day. In general, daytime concerts begin at 10:30 A.M. on Saturdays (these are rehearsals) and 2:30 P.M. on Sundays. Concerts last about two hours.

A few miles south of Pittsfield is the gracious town of Lenox, which, along with neighboring Stockbridge, contains the largest concentration of grand estates in the Berkshires. Most of the estates were built in the late 1800s as summer "cottages" for financial and industrial tycoons. A few were built for artists, writers, and political figures. These buildings live on today as museums, schools, centers for the performing arts, and resorts. Cycling past these noble structures, the lovely town center of Lenox, and rich farmland in the outlying areas is pure pleasure as long as you're not fighting for roadspace with Tanglewood traffic.

The ride starts about ⁷/₁₀ mile south of the center of Pittsfield and heads south through an attractive residential area on secondary roads. Shortly before the Lenox town line you'll pass Arrowhead, an eighteenth-century farmhouse where Herman Melville lived from 1850 to 1863. The house, including the studio where he wrote *Moby Dick*, is open to the public. There's a good view of Mount Greylock, about 15 miles to the north, from the meadow next to the house. Continuing south past farms with mountain views in the background, you'll come to the first estate, Eastover (now a resort), after about 3 miles.

Beyond Eastover, the route rolls up and down and then descends gradually to the Housatonic River, which flows from Pittsfield to Long Island Sound near Bridgeport, Connecticut. The graceful former Lenox train station, built in 1902, stands on the riverbank. It is now a railroad museum and the locale of the Berkshire Scenic Railway, which offers short train rides on an old passenger car. You'll follow the river through the quiet village of Lenoxdale, passing a fine wooden church and a handsome stucco school building that has been tastefully converted into apartments.

From Lenoxdale you'll climb gradually away from the river, passing four grand estates within 2 miles. The first one is Blantyre, an exclusive, very private resort built in the style of a Scottish manor. Just ahead is Cranwell, now a resort, conference center, and golf club. The Berkshire Opera Company performs in its round, boldly architectured auditorium. Next you'll come to The Mount, the splendid summer mansion of Edith Wharton, the first woman to win a Pulitzer Prize. The theater group Shakespeare and Company performs on the grounds of the estate. Finally you'll pass Canyon Ranch, a health spa that was formerly an estate called Bellefontaine, built in the style of a French palace. (There are no canyons nearby—the name comes from the original spa in Tucson, Arizona.)

Shortly after the Canyon Ranch, you'll arrive at the classically elegant center of Lenox. It is dominated by the Curtis, a brick, four-story former hotel that has been converted into apartments. Next to it is the graceful Lenox Library, originally built in 1815 as a courthouse. The handsome, pillared town hall stands across the street from the Curtis. Surrounding the center of town are large wooden houses with gabled roofs and wide porches, most of them converted into inns.

From the center of Lenox, a descent leads to the main entrance to Tanglewood, the summer home of the Boston Symphony Orchestra. The entrance is in Lenox, but the actual performance area, called the Shed, is in Stockbridge. You may walk (not ride) through the grounds when there are no concerts scheduled. The toughest hill on the ride comes up shortly after Tanglewood, but you can take a break near the top at an overlook that provides a magnificent view of Stockbridge Bowl, a lake just south of Tanglewood rimmed by mountains. A steep descent leads into a fertile valley. The rest of the ride winds through rolling farmland, and you'll pass an apple and cider store about 5 miles from the end.

The short ride bypasses most of the estates and the Tanglewood area by heading directly into the center of Lenox before reaching the railroad station, and then following a more direct route from Lenox back to Pittsfield. You'll pass the classically elegant Church on the Hill, built in 1805, a half mile outside of town.

The center of Pittsfield is worth a visit. The Berkshire Athenaeum (the public library), with an outstanding Melville collection, is excellent. Just south of Park Square is the Berkshire Museum, with exhibits of art, local history, artifacts, and natural history. The Lichtenstein Center for the Arts (28 Renne Avenue, 2 blocks north of Park Square and 1 block east of North Street) is a municipal arts center with studios, workshops, and exhibits.

Directions for the ride: 25 miles

1. Jog left on South Street and immediately right on Crofut Street, at traffic light. Go $3/10$ mile to end (Pomeroy Avenue).
2. Turn right on Pomeroy Avenue and go $9/10$ mile to end (Holmes Road).
3. Turn right at end and go $1\frac{1}{2}$ miles to Chapman Street on left, opposite Tamie Way on right. You'll pass Arrowhead (Herman Meville's home) on your right after 1 mile, at top of hill.
4. Turn left on Chapman Street and go $37/10$ miles to crossroads and stop sign (Housatonic Street). Chapman Street becomes East Street at the Lenox town line. You'll enjoy views of the mountains on your left. The Eastover resort is on the left after $27/10$ miles. The short ride turns right on Housatonic Street, and the long ride turns left.
5. Turn left on Housatonic Street and go $8/10$ mile to crossroads where the main road turns right. Here the ride turns right, but if you go left and continue 50 yards, you'll see the Lenox railroad station and Berkshire Scenic Railway on the right.
6. Turn right on main road. Go $12/10$ miles to fork where Mill Street turns left across a bridge and the main road curves right. **CAUTION:** Watch for potholes and cracks. You'll ride through Lenoxdale, passing the former Crystal Hill School (now apartments) and a graceful brown church on the right.
7. Bear right at fork, passing small brick church on left. Go $6/10$ mile to crossroads (East Street on right, Blantyre Road on left), just after top of hill.

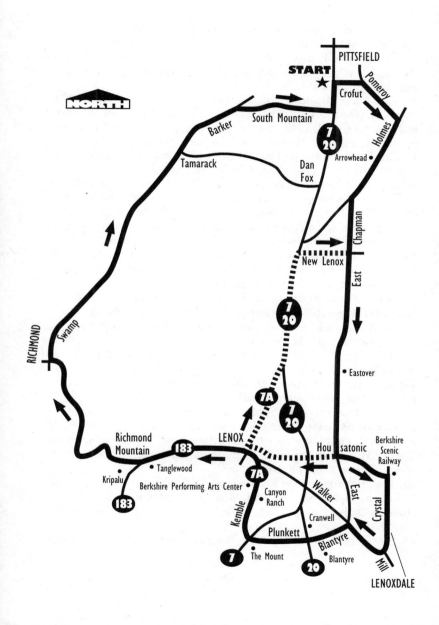

8. Turn left at crossroads and go $^6/_{10}$ mile to Route 20, at stop sign. On your left, hidden behind gatehouses and woods, is Blantyre, a former grand estate that is now an exclusive inn (the grounds are not open to the public). When you get to Route 20 you'll see Cranwell, another former estate that is worth a look, on the right.

9. Cross Route 20 and go $^9/_{10}$ mile to traffic light (Route 7). There are sweeping views to the left. You'll pass The Mount (Edith Wharton's home and the locale of Shakespeare and Company) on the left immediately before the light. The mansion is set back $^3/_{10}$ mile from the road.

10. Cross Route 7 and go $1^4/_{10}$ miles to end, at stop sign (Walker Street, unmarked). You'll pass Canyon Ranch (a former estate that is now a health spa) on the right and the National Music Center (also called the Berkshire Performing Arts Center; it was formerly a boys' school) on the left. At the end, notice the handsome stone church on the right.

11. Turn left at end and go $^2/_{10}$ mile to monument in the center of Lenox. At the monument the former Curtis Hotel (now apartments) is on your right, and the town hall is on your left. Here the ride bears left onto Route 183, but if you bear right on Route 7A and go 100 yards you'll see the Lenox Library, built in 1815, on the right.

12. Bear left at monument onto Route 183. Go $1^1/_2$ miles to fork where Richmond Mountain Road bears right (sign points to Route 41, Richmond).

You'll enjoy a long, steady descent out of Lenox. The main entrance to Tanglewood is on the left just before the fork, and the entrance to the Kripalu Center for Yoga and Health (formerly a Jesuit monastery) is immediately after it.

13. Bear right on Richmond Mountain Road and go $3^2/_{10}$ miles to crossroads and stop sign (Swamp Road).

You'll climb steeply at the beginning, level off, and then climb steeply once more. As you're making the second ascent, an overlook on the left provides a stunning view of Stockbridge Bowl far below, with Rattlesnake Hill rising behind it. After cresting the summit, you'll descend very steeply on a smooth road.

14. Turn right on Swamp Road and go $5^4/_{10}$ miles to fork where Barker Road bears slightly left and South Mountain Road bears right. You'll pass Bartlett's Orchard, an excellent apple and cider store, on the right after $2^4/_{10}$ miles.

15. Bear right on South Mountain Road and go $1^1/_2$ miles to end (South

Street, Routes 7 and 20). You'll skirt the base of South Mountain on your right.

16. Turn left on South Street and go ½ mile to Taylor Street on left, immediately before traffic light.

Directions for the ride: 15 miles ◁◦◁◦◁◦◁◦◁◦◁◦

1. Follow directions for the long ride through number 4.

2. Turn right on Housatonic Street and go ½ mile to traffic light (Routes 7 and 20). This is a gradual climb.

3. Continue straight for ⁸⁄₁₀ mile to crossroads (Church Street). A one-way street in the wrong direction is straight ahead. You'll pass an attractive brick school on the right.

4. Turn left on Church Street and go ¹⁄₁₀ mile to end (Walker Street, unmarked). Here the ride turns right, but if you turn left and go 200 yards you'll pass several gracious old mansions, now inns, on your left.

5. Turn right at end and go ¹⁄₁₀ mile to monument in the center of Lenox (Route 7A bears right here). The former Curtis Hotel (now apartments) is on the right at the intersection, and the town hall is on the left.

6. Bear right on Route 7A and go 1²⁄₁₀ miles to yield sign (merge left on Routes 7 and 20). The Lenox Library, built in 1815, is on the right immediately after the Curtis. The Federal-style Lenox Academy, built in 1805, is on the left just past the library. The picturesque Church on the Hill, also built in 1805, is on the left ³⁄₁₀ mile beyond the Academy.

7. Bear left on Routes 7 and 20 (**CAUTION** here) and go 1⁸⁄₁₀ miles to New Lenox Road on right.

8. Turn right on New Lenox Road and go ⁸⁄₁₀ to crossroads and stop sign (East Street).

9. Turn left on East Street and go ⁹⁄₁₀ mile to crossroads and stop sign (Holmes Road, unmarked).

10. Turn right on Holmes Road and go 1½ miles to Pomeroy Avenue on left. If you come to a small bridge over the Housatonic River, you've gone ¹⁄₁₀ mile too far. The Canoe Meadows Audubon Sanctuary is just past the intersection on the right.

11. Turn left on Pomeroy Avenue and go ⁹⁄₁₀ mile to Crofut Street on left. Pomeroy Avenue bears right at the intersection.

12. Turn left on Crofut Street and go ³⁄₁₀ mile to end (Routes 7 and 20).

13. Jog left at end and immediately right on Taylor Street.

Mansions, Mills, Mountains, Museums, Music, and Meditation:
Housatonic–Stockbridge–Lenox

Number of miles: 23 (13 without Lenox extension)
Terrain: The short ride is gently rolling. The long ride is fairly hilly, with several short, steep climbs and two long, steady ones.
Food: Restaurants and grocery stores in the towns.
Start: Monument Mountain Reservation, Route 7, Great Barrington. It's about halfway between the center of that town and Stockbridge, on the west side of the road.

CAUTION:
The long ride goes past Tanglewood, which breeds traffic jams on the narrow nearby roads before and after concerts. See **CAUTION** notice for ride 5 for more information.

The neighboring towns of Stockbridge and Lenox, about 5 to 10 miles south of Pittsfield, boast the largest concentration of estates and cultural attractions in the Berkshires. The centers of both towns are elegant—the traditional New England townscape at its finest, graced with handsome churches, inns, libraries, and town halls. In contrast, Housatonic is a mill town with a wonderful example of Victorian industrial architecture. The region's well-maintained secondary roads, winding past mansions and estates with mountain views across their extensive lawns, promise bicycling at its best.

The ride starts from Monument Mountain Reservation, a natural area maintained by the Trustees of Reservations. Two hiking trails lead to the summit of the mountain, a narrow ridge with distinctive rocky cliffs. The view from the top, about 800 feet above the surrounding valleys, is spectacular. At the beginning of the ride you'll descend gradually to the Housatonic River and pass the splendid brick mill of the Rising Paper Company, adorned with graceful towers and built in 1876. About a mile ahead is the center of Housatonic, a small mill town (part of Great Barrington) that has seen better days, but it has begun to rebound as a center for artists and craftspeople who have set up studios in the cavernous brick and stone mills along the river. A fine brick church and a handsome library grace the center of town.

From Housatonic you'll follow the river of the same name into the outskirts of Stockbridge. After about 3 miles, you may detour a short way off the route to visit Chesterwood, the summer home and studio of sculptor Daniel Chester French from 1898 to 1931. French's most famous works are the statue of Abraham Lincoln at the Lincoln Memorial in Washington, D.C., and the statue of the minuteman in Concord. Just ahead is the wonderful Norman Rockwell Museum, which moved in 1993 from the center of Stockbridge to more spacious quarters on the grounds of a former estate outside of town. Rockwell, loved for his incredibly realistic illustrations of everyday American life, lived in Stockbridge from 1953 until he died in 1978. Shortly beyond the museum is the lovely Berkshire Botanical Garden, with displays of flowers, herbs, and shrubs.

At this point the short ride turns east, heading toward the center of Stockbridge. Stockbridge is the quintessential traditional New England town. It became famous in the 1930s as the locale of the Berkshire Theater Festival and of the Tanglewood Music Festival, and later as the setting for many of Norman Rockwell's illustrations. In 1967 Stockbridge received another boost of fame as the scene of Arlo Guthrie's adventures, described in his narrative ballad (and movie two years later), "Alice's Restaurant." The song became an anthem for the hippie era and the movement against the draft during the Vietnam War. Shortly before the center of town you'll see the tall, brick Congregational Church, a graceful clock tower (called the Children's Chimes) in front of it, and the handsome pillared town hall next door. Just ahead are two historic houses. The Merwin House, dating from around 1825, is a brick, Federal-style gem with period furnishings. The Mission House, built in 1739, is a weathered frame house built by John Sergeant, the first missionary to the local Indians.

Just beyond the Mission House is the town's main intersection, dominated by the rambling, four-story Red Lion Inn. A handsome row of ornate Victorian buildings, now mainly shops and boutiques, stands next to the inn, and a dignified stone church guards the opposite corner. Another Stockbridge landmark ($^6/_{10}$ mile off the route, east of town on

Route 7) is the Berkshire Theater Festival headquarters, a graceful wooden building designed by Stanford White in 1889. From the Red Lion Inn it's 3 miles back to the starting point. You'll pass the old train station, now vacant, just outside of town.

The long ride continues north at the Berkshire Botanical Garden toward Lenox and loops back into the center of Stockbridge farther along the route. You'll go through the tiny village of Interlaken (part of Stockbridge), passing a graceful brick church. About 2 miles farther on you'll catch glimpses of Stockbridge Bowl (also called Lake Mahkeenac), a beautiful clear lake surrounded by mountains and set back from the road. Just ahead is one of the Berkshires' more unusual landmarks, the Kripalu Center for Yoga and Health. Kripalu (accented on the second syllable) is a center for self-discovery, holistic health, meditation, and spiritual enrichment situated on a broad hillside with a splendid view of Stockbridge Bowl and the mountains beyond. The site originally boasted Shadowbrook, the grandest of the Berkshire estates. After that dwelling burned down in 1956, the surprisingly unattractive current building was constructed as a Jesuit monastery.

Just beyond Kripalu is the main entrance to Tanglewood, the summer home of the Boston Symphony Orchestra since 1936. The performance area (called the Shed) is in Stockbridge, but the entrance is in Lenox. You may walk (not ride) around the beautifully landscaped grounds, with mountain views in the distance, if there is no concert scheduled. From Tanglewood it's about a mile and a half to the center of Lenox, with the last ¾ mile going steadily uphill.

Like Stockbridge, Lenox is an archetypal gracious New England town. The center of town is dominated by the Curtis, a four-story, brick former hotel that has been tastefully recycled into apartments. Next to the Curtis is the Lenox Library, framed by tall columns and a graceful cupola. It was built in 1815 as a courthouse. The handsome brick town hall stands across the street from the Curtis. You'll descend steeply out of town past gracious old houses, some of which are now inns. About a mile out of town, just over the Stockbridge line, you'll pass Wheatleigh, a former estate that is now an elegant hotel. (The name is English, but the architecture is Italian Renaissance.) Just ahead the road dips down to the shore of Stockbridge Bowl, a lake rimmed by mountains, and then it climbs onto a hillside past mansions with mountain views.

A steep descent brings you into the center of Stockbridge, but it's

Kripalu
Tanglewood
183
LENOX
Old Stockbridge
Hawthorne Rd.
Hawthorne St.
Wheatleigh
Stockbridge Bowl
Interlaken Crossroad
Willard Hill
INTERLAKEN
Trask
183
Prospect Hill
NORTH
Berkshire Botanical Garden
102
Norman Rockwell Museum
Naumkeag
Chesterwood
Pine
Marian Shrine
STOCKBRIDGE
Glendale Middle Rd.
102
7
183
Housatonic River
Main
7
HOUSATONIC
START
Rising Mill
183

worth interrupting it to see two more attractions across the road from each other. Naumkeag is a gracious, gabled mansion designed by Stanford White in 1885 and now maintained by the Trustees of Reservations. It served as the summer estate of Joseph Hodges Choate, a prominent attorney and ambassador to England. Across the road is Eden Hill, a shrine and monastery of the Marians of the Immaculate Conception. The ornate stone chapel (open to visitors), set amidst rolling fields, was built by hand between 1950 and 1960, but it looks like it was transplanted from Central Europe 500 years ago.

When you arrive in the center of town, you'll make a brief out-and-back excursion past the Mission House, the Merwin House, the Congregational Church and clock tower in front of it, and the town hall. From the Red Lion Inn it's a flat, smooth 3 miles back to the starting point.

Directions for the ride: 23 miles 〰〰〰〰〰

1. Turn right (south) on Route 7 and go $^8/_{10}$ mile to the first right (unmarked).
2. Turn right on this road and go $^1/_2$ mile to end, at stop sign (merge left on Route 183). You will turn sharply right here.
3. Turn sharply right on Route 183. Go $2^3/_{10}$ miles to crossroads where Route 183 turns right, in Housatonic. It's immediately after you go under a railroad bridge. You'll pass the Rising Paper Mill, built in 1876, on the left and then ride along the dammed-up Housatonic River.
4. Continue straight at crossroads for $^1/_{10}$ mile to end (Main Street).
5. Turn right on Main Street and go $^3/_{10}$ mile to end (Route 183 again). You'll pass an attractive brick church and stately library on the left.
6. Turn left on Route 183 and go $2^6/_{10}$ miles to crossroads where Glendale Middle Road turns right and Christian Hill Road turns left.

You'll follow the river on your right. When you get to the crossroads, the ride goes straight, but if you'd like to visit Chesterwood (Daniel Chester French's home and studio), turn left on Christian Hill Road and go $^3/_{10}$ mile to end. Turn left again and go $^3/_{10}$ mile to Chesterwood on right. The last $^1/_{10}$ mile is dirt road.
7. Continue on Route 183 for $1^3/_{10}$ miles to Route 102, at blinking light. Here the short ride turns right and the long ride goes straight. The Norman Rockwell Museum is on your right after $^1/_2$ mile; it's about $^1/_4$ mile off the road. To see the Berkshire Botanical Garden, turn left on Route

102 and go $^1/_{10}$ mile to the garden on left.

8. Cross Route 102 and go 1 mile to Trask Lane on right, as you come into the village of Interlaken.

9. Turn right on Trask Lane and go 100 yards to Willard Hill Road (unmarked) on left. Hill Road bears right at the intersection.

10. Turn left on Willard Hill Road and go $^3/_{10}$ mile to end (merge left at large, grassy traffic island). The graceful brick Congregational church is on the right at the top of the hill. Immediately after the church you'll see the Interlaken School of Art, an ornate Victorian mansion with a central tower, on the left.

11. Bear left at end and go 100 yards to stop sign (merge right on Route 183).

12. Bear right on Route 183 and go $4^1/_{10}$ miles to crossroads in the center of Lenox, at top of hill.

After $2^1/_{10}$ miles you'll pass the Kripalu Center for Yoga and Health on the left. There's a stunning view of Stockbridge Bowl, with Rattlesnake Hill rising behind it, from in front of the main building. The main entrance to Tanglewood is $^6/_{10}$ mile past Kripalu. There's a long, steady climb into Lenox. When you arrive in the center of town the Curtis, an attractive brick hotel recycled into apartments, is on the far left corner. The elegant Lenox Library is next to it, and the imposing brick town hall is on the far right corner.

13. Turn right in the center of Lenox onto Old Stockbridge Road. Go $^3/_{10}$ mile to Hawthorne Street on right, at bottom of steep part of hill.

14. Turn right on Hawthorne Street and go $1^2/_{10}$ miles to end (Hawthorne Road), passing large, gracious homes.

15. Turn left on Hawthorne Road and go $4^7/_{10}$ miles to crossroads and stop sign (Route 102), in the center of Stockbridge. After $^2/_{10}$ mile you'll pass Wheatleigh on the left, tucked out of sight off the road. A half mile ahead you'll ride along Stockbridge Bowl on your right. The large building on the far side of the lake is the Kripalu Center. About 3 miles beyond Stockbridge Bowl you'll pass Naumkeag on the right, opposite the entrance to Eden Hill (the Marian shrine) on the left. The lovely chapel is $^3/_{10}$ mile off the road.

When you get to Route 102, notice the handsome stone church on your left. The Red Lion Inn is on the far left corner. The ornate brick building two doors to the left of the inn was built in 1884 as the town hall; it now contains shops.

16. Turn right on Route 102, go ⁴/₁₀ mile to where Route 102 turns right, and backtrack to crossroads.

This brief out-and-back stretch is too special to omit from the ride. The entire way is lined with elegant houses, estates, and other buildings. You'll pass the Mission House (1739) on the right and the Merwin House (c. 1825) on the left. Just ahead on the left, at the point where you make the U-turn, you'll see the impressive town hall and the brick Congregational Church. The graceful Children's Chimes clock tower stands in front of the church.

17. Turn right at crossroads onto Route 7 South, passing the Red Lion Inn on your left. Go 3 miles to starting point on right. After ³/₁₀ mile you'll pass the old train station, now vacant, on your left. It was designed by Stanford White and built in 1893.

Directions for the ride: 13 miles 〜〜〜〜〜〜〜〜

1. Follow directions for the long ride through number 7.

2. Turn right on Route 102 and go 1⁴/₁₀ miles to end (Route 102 turns left). The handsome brick Congregational Church is in front of you at the intersection, with the white-pillared town hall next to the church on the left. The graceful Children's Chimes clock tower stands in front of the church.

3. Turn left (still Route 102) and go ⁴/₁₀ mile to crossroads in the center of Stockbridge where Route 7 South turns right. This section is lined with elegant houses and estates. You'll pass the Merwin House (c. 1825) on the right and the Mission House (1739) on the left. When you get to the crossroads, the Red Lion Inn is on the far right corner and a handsome stone church is on the far left corner. Here the ride turns right, but it is worth continuing straight for 1 block to see the wonderful row of Victorian buildings immediately after the Inn. The brick, step-gabled former town hall, built in 1884, is especially striking; it now contains shops.

4. Follow direction number 17 of the long ride.

West Stockbridge–
Great Barrington–Alford

Number of miles: 25

Terrain: Rolling, with several steep climbs.

Food: Grocery and restaurants in Great Barrington, country store and restaurant in West Stockbridge, near end.

Start: Village school on Route 102 in West Stockbridge, ½ mile west of the center of town. Park at the ball field on the right-hand side of the school.

How to get there: From the west, take the Berkshire extension of the New York State Thruway (I–90) to exit B-3 (Route 22). Turn left at end of ramp and immediately right on Route 22 South. Go ⁷⁄₁₀ mile to Route 102 on left. Turn left on Route 102 and go 2½ miles to school on right.

From the east, take the Massachusetts Turnpike to exit 1, immediately after toll booth. Turn right at end of ramp, and just ahead turn left at end on Route 102. Follow Route 102 for ⁸⁄₁₀ mile to school on left.

The western edge of Massachusetts, about a third of the way between the state's southern and northern borders, provides spectacular bicycling through a landscape of farms and meadows, with wooded hills and mountains rising abruptly on the horizon. The classic New England villages of West Stockbridge and Alford, along with the handsome commercial town of Great Barrington, add variety to the serenely rural area.

The beginning of the ride passes through West Stockbridge, which is not as well known and much less visited than neighboring Stockbridge, 5 miles to the southeast. The center of the village contains shops and eateries in old wooden buildings and a former train station that now houses retail establishments. You'll follow Route 41, a gently rolling secondary road with light traffic, for nearly 10 miles to the outskirts of Great Barrington. Midway along this stretch is the hamlet of WIlliamsville (part of West Stockbridge), where you'll ride past the Williamsville Inn, a traditional New England hostelry in a rambling wooden building. Beyond Williamsville the countryside becomes more open, and you'll enjoy views of hills rising behind dairy farms.

Great Barrington, the largest town in southwestern Massachusetts, seems bigger than a community of 7,500. The bustling downtown area boasts several impressive churches and a business district with handsome, three-story brick buildings from the late 1800s. The Searles Castle, a 40-room stone mansion built during the 1880s by the widow of railroad tycoon Mark Hopkins, is a downtown landmark. It is now the John Dewey Academy, a school for teenagers with emotional problems. A tough, $7/10$-mile-long hill greets you as you leave Great Barrington. About 2 miles out of town is tiny Simon's Rock College, with about 300 students. The college, which enrolls many of its students after their sophomore or junior year of high school, emphasizes seminar-style education and close relationships between students and faculty. The starkly modern campus is set back about $3/10$ mile from the road.

The picture-book hamlet of Alford—with a graceful church, elegant town hall, and rustic little schoolhouse, all in traditional New England white—is about 3 miles beyond the college. Most of the return trip from Alford back to West Stockbridge follows a beckoning country road that rolls up and down through farmland, with forested hills and mountains in the distance.

Directions for the ride

1. Turn right (east) on Route 102 and go less than $2/10$ mile to end (merge right at stop sign).

2. Bear right (still Route 102) and go $6/10$ mile to Route 41 on right, at top of hill. You'll go through the center of West Stockbridge.

3. Turn right on Route 41 and go $9\frac{1}{2}$ miles to stop sign (merge right on Route 7), on the outskirts of Great Barrington. **CAUTION:** Watch for potholes.

This long stretch is gently rolling. The first $4\frac{1}{2}$ miles, to the hamlet of Williamsville, are mostly wooded. Then the landscape opens up, and you'll enjoy views of the hills on your left.

4. Bear right on Route 7 and go $7/10$ mile to Taconic Avenue on right, at traffic light, just past the business district. **CAUTION:** The downtown area is very busy on summer weekends—watch for parked cars pulling out, car doors opening in front of you, and pedestrians.

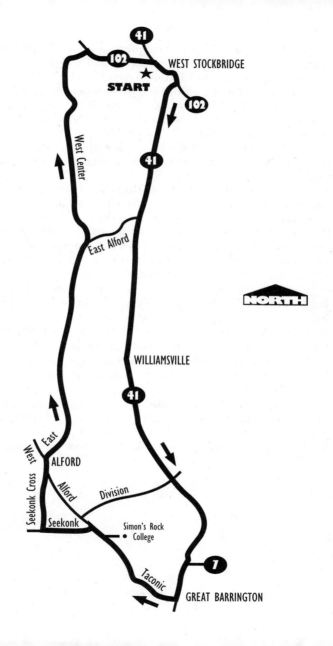

You'll pass two handsome stone churches on your left just before the center of town. Searles Castle, hidden behind a high stone wall, is on your left when you come to Taconic Avenue.

5. Turn right on Taconic Avenue and go $\frac{1}{10}$ mile to where the main road bears left, immediately after you go underneath a railroad bridge.

6. Bear left on main road and go $2\frac{1}{10}$ miles to Seekonk Road on left, shortly after Simon's Rock College on right.

You'll have a steady climb of $\frac{7}{10}$ mile at the beginning, with a steep section near the top. Farther on there's another steady hill that's $\frac{4}{10}$ mile long.

7. Turn left on Seekonk Road. **CAUTION:** Metal-plate bridge as soon as you turn; walk across if the road is wet. Go $1\frac{1}{10}$ miles to Seekonk Cross Road on right, just as you start to climb a steep hill.

8. Turn right on Seekonk Cross Road and go $1\frac{2}{10}$ miles to end, at stop sign (merge left at bottom of hill). You'll climb steeply onto a ridge with fine views. Just before the end you'll see the distinctive hump of Tom Ball Mountain in front of you to the right.

9. Bear left at end and go $\frac{2}{10}$ mile to fork in the center of Alford (West Road bears left, East Road bears right). A traditional white church and little wooden school stand in the middle of the fork.

10. Bear right on East Road and go $4\frac{1}{10}$ miles to fork where East Alford Road bears right and West Center Road bears left.

In the first mile you'll have two steep climbs, each about $\frac{2}{10}$ mile long. After the second hill, the road rolls up and down through rich farmland with glorious views.

11. Bear left on West Center Road and go 4 miles to end (Route 102), The superb scenery continues, with the last mile heading mostly downhill.

12. Turn right on Route 102 and go $1\frac{1}{10}$ miles to school on right.

Lee–Otis–Monterey–Tyringham

Number of miles: 29
Terrain: Hilly.
Food: Country stores in Otis and Monterey. Burger King at end.
Start: Burger King, Route 20 in Lee, just west of exit 2 of the Massachusetts Turnpike.

This ride makes a circuit of a town and three small villages in the southeastern part of Berkshire County. Unlike the elegant, estate-sprinkled towns of Lenox and Stockbridge to the north, the communities on this ride are workaday farming villages that have hardly changed in generations, with traditional white churches, weathered graveyards, and appealing country stores that aren't filled with tourists. The route winds through primarily wooded countryside (with the lovely, open Tyringham Valley for contrast), passing several ponds along the way.

The ride starts from Lee, a small town with a handsome brick business block and a tall white church. (The center of town is about a mile northwest of the starting point on Route 20.) As you head east out of town, you'll climb gradually into the surrounding hills, passing Greenwater Pond, with rustic cottages along its shore, and then Shaw Pond. Shortly before Otis you'll pass a poultry farm with a bit of folk wisdom written on a row of chicken coops. Otis is typical of the smaller Berkshire communities off the tourist path, with a lovely white church and a small general store that serves nearly as much as a community center as a place to shop.

From Otis the route winds up and down to Monterey, another village with some handsome old houses, a white church, and an inviting country store with a bulletin board out front and old wooden benches on the porch. Outside of town, just off the route, you can visit Joyous Springs Pottery, where pottery is crafted using traditional Japanese methods. A little farther off the route on the same road is the Bidwell House, a handsome white farmhouse built around 1750 and filled with period furnishings. The route plunges steeply for a mile and a half—fortunately the road is smooth—and suddenly you enter the Tyringham Valley, a broad expanse of soft green fields and meadows with wooded hills rising behind them. The tiny hamlet of Tyringham, with only a few lovely wooden houses, a white church with a small cemetery behind it, and an attractive stone library-plus-post office, lies on the edge of the valley.

Just beyond the village you'll pass the architectural highlight of the ride, the Tyringham Art Galleries (also called the Gingerbread House or the Witch House). It is a cottage that consists primarily of a thick, waving roof, designed to resemble thatch and evoke the spirit of the rolling hills. It was built in 1916 by sculptor Henry Kitson, best known for his statue of the minuteman in Lexington, and it served as his studio for many years. From the Galleries it's about 3 miles back to the starting point.

Directions for the ride 🌾🌾🌾🌾🌾🌾🌾🌾🌾🌾🌾🌾

1. Turn right (east) on Route 20 and go ³/₁₀ mile to traffic light where Route 20 East curves left.
2. Continue on Route 20 East for 6⁷/₁₀ miles to fork where Routes 8 North and 20 East bear left, and Route 8 South goes straight.

For the first 2 miles you'll climb gradually, with one steeper section near the top. After ⁸/₁₀ mile, notice the handsome Victorian house on your left. You'll ride along Greenwater Pond on the right about 4 miles farther on.
3. Go straight at fork onto Route 8 South. Go 5⁶/₁₀ miles to Route 23 West, which turns sharply right as you come into Otis.

You'll pass the Egg Factory Outlet Store on the left after 2⁷/₁₀ miles; the message "Egg eaters make better lovers" is written on a row of little red sheds. When you get to Route 23 West the ride turns right, but if you continue straight you'll reach the center of Otis just ahead, with a country store on the right.
4. Turn sharply right on Route 23 West and go 7¹/₁₀ miles to Tyringham Road on the right, in the center of Monterey. It's immediately before the country store on the left. (You'll pass another Tyringham Road on the right after about 3¹/₂ miles; go straight here.)

A small, Gothic-style church and hillside cemetery are on your left as you turn onto Route 23. You'll climb steadily out of Otis, with three

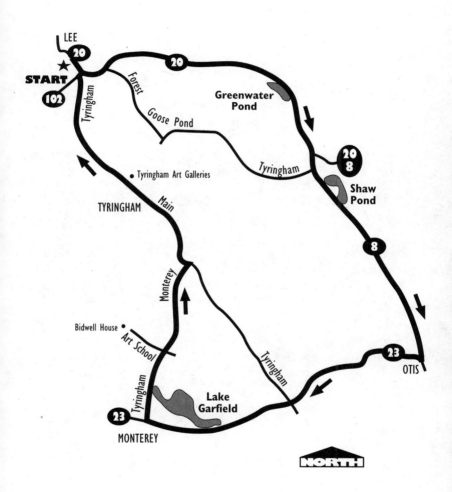

Tyringham Art Galleries

short, steep pitches. Royal Pond is on the left at the Monterey town line. The ride turns right in Monterey, but Bidwell Park is just past the intersection on the left. Here the Konkapot River flows over a small dam; it's a good spot to enjoy the snack you bought at the country store.

5. Turn right in Monterey and go 3⁸/10 miles to end.

You'll pass Lake Garfield on the right after ³/4 mile, and then come to a crossroads ⁷/10 mile beyond the lake (Mount Hunger Road on right; Art School Road on left). If you turn left here, Joyous Springs Pottery will be on the right after ²/10 mile, and the Bidwell House is ⁸/10 mile farther on (it's a steady climb on a dirt road).

The long, steep descent into the Tyringham Valley begins ⁴/10 mile beyond the crossroads. Fortunately the road is smooth, but **CAUTION—** keep your speed under control.

6. Turn left at end and go 5¹/2 miles to end (Route 102; sign may say TO ROUTE 20). The road follows the Tyringham Valley on your left. You'll come into the center of Tyringham after 1⁴/10 miles, and the Tyringham Art Galleries (the Gingerbread House) will be on the right ⁸/10 mile farther on.

7. Turn right on Route 102 and go 100 yards to Route 20 West on left.

8. Turn left on Route 20 West and immediately curve left at traffic light (still Route 20 West). Go ³/10 mile to Burger King on left.

Antique Alley:
Great Barrington–Sheffield–
Ashley Falls–South Egremont

Number of miles: 29 (17 without Ashley Falls extension)
Terrain: Gently rolling, with one moderate hill and one steep one.
Food: Grocery and snack bar in Sheffield and South Egremont.
Start: Shopping center on Route 7 in Great Barrington, 1 mile south of the center of town and 6/10 mile south of Route 23 west.

The southwestern corner of Massachusetts abounds with elegant villages and fertile farmland, with views of gently rounded Mount Everett, the second-highest mountain in the Berkshires with an elevation of 2,602 feet, in the distance. The valleys near the Connecticut state line are broad and flat, providing some of the easiest bicycling in Berkshire County. If you like antiques, you're in the right place—the villages of Sheffield and South Egremont boast the highest concentration of antiques shops (most of them in handsome wooden, stone, or brick houses about 200 years old) in the state. The long ride goes by Bartholomew's Cobble, a rocky hill overlooking the Housatonic River with wonderful views.

Starting from the southern edge of Great Barrington, the ride follows a back road through the nearly level valley of the Housatonic River, passing dairy farms that extend to the river's edge. After about 6 miles you'll come to Sheffield and pass dozens of antiques shops on Route 7, the only busy road on the ride (fortunately, it has a wide shoulder). From Sheffield, the route continues along the valley past more dairy farms to the crossroads hamlet of Ashley Falls, where you'll see several more antiques shops in fine old houses. About a mile beyond Ashley Falls is the scenic highlight of the ride, Bartholomew's Cobble, which consists of a pair of small rocky outcroppings that rise about 100 feet above the Housatonic River. Foot trails lead about 100 yards to the first hill and 1/4 mile to the second one, affording panoramic views of the meandering river below and mountains in the distance. Just beyond Bartholomew's Cobble is the Colonel Ashley House, the oldest house in Berkshire

County, built in 1735. Both the Cobble and the Colonel Ashley House have modest admission fees.

Just past the Colonel Ashley House, you'll ascend the only tough hill on the ride and cross into Salisbury, Connecticut for about 4 miles. Shortly beyond the state line you'll pass the conference center of the Institute of World Affairs, a nonpartisan organization devoted to international understanding and the peaceful resolution of conflict. The hamlet of Taconic, where the main building is the post office, is about a mile farther on. As you reenter Massachusetts, you'll pass the Option Institute and Fellowship, a former estate that is now a facility for personal and emotional growth. It also houses a center for children with special needs, with an emphasis on autism.

The ride now heads north to South Egremont along Route 41, a beautiful secondary road with the rugged Mount Washington Range (of which Mount Everett is the highest peak) on your left, and farms and meadows on your right. You'll pass the handsome brick Stagecoach Hill Inn and then the Berkshire School, a top-quality, coeducational prep school with elegant stone buildings nestled at the foot of Mount Bushnell. South Egremont is a traditional New England village with several antiques shops, the Egremont Inn built in 1780, and a unique little library dating from 1830. The final section back to Great Barrington passes through sweeping expanses of farmland bordered by wooded hills. Shortly before the end you'll see an unusual statue of a newsboy hawking a newspaper; it was built in 1895 by one of the owners of the *New York Daily News*.

The short ride heads west from Sheffield on a flat road with good views of Mount Everett at its far end and rejoins the long ride shortly before the Berkshire School.

Directions for the ride: 29 miles

1. Turn right (south) on Route 7 and go ³⁄₁₀ mile to Brookside Road on left (sign may say TO JOSEPH EISNER CAMP INSTITUTE).
2. Turn left on Brookside Road and go ¼ mile to East Sheffield Road on right. The Joseph Eisner Camp Institute, a Jewish summer camp, is on your left at the intersection.
3. Turn right on East Sheffield Road and go 4⁹⁄₁₀ miles to end (Maple Avenue). **CAUTION:** Watch for potholes for the first mile, up to the Sheffield

town line. You'll follow the Housatonic River closely at the beginning. Then you'll ride past prosperous dairy farms lying between the road and the river, with good views of Mount Everett on your right.

4. Turn right on Maple Avenue and go $^8/_{10}$ mile to end (Route 7), in Sheffield.

5. Turn left on Route 7 and go $^4/_{10}$ mile to Berkshire School Road on right. Here the short ride turns right and the long ride goes straight. You'll go through the center of Sheffield, passing a grocery and snack bar on your right and several antiques shops.

6. Continue straight on Route 7 for $1^4/_{10}$ miles to fork where Route 7 bears left and Route 7A bears right. You'll pedal past numerous antiques shops. Route 7 and the next two roads are nearly as flat as a pancake—enjoy the terrain while it lasts.

7. Bear right on Route 7A and go $2^4/_{10}$ miles to crossroads and blinking light (East Main Street on left, Rannapo Road on right). This is Ashley Falls, a village in Sheffield.

8. Turn right at crossroads and go 1 mile to fork where Rannapo Road bears right and Cooper Hill Road bears left. You'll see Mount Everett in front of you.

Just before the fork, a dirt road on the left leads $^1/_{10}$ mile to the entrance to Bartholomew's Cobble, which is worth a stop. It's only a five-minute walk to the top of the closest hill and back along Eaton Trail. Other trails lead along the Housatonic River and up the next hill.

9. Bear left on Cooper Hill Road and go $1^2/_{10}$ miles to end (merge left at yield sign). The Colonel Ashley House is on your left near the beginning, and you'll have wonderful views of mountains rising behind farmland. Then you'll climb very steeply for $^3/_{10}$ mile toward the end—the toughest hill of the ride.

10. Bear left at end and go $2^3/_{10}$ miles to fork at a large triangular traffic island (or a small green—take your pick), in the hamlet of Taconic, which is part of Salisbury, Connecticut. You'll cross into Connecticut after $^3/_{10}$ mile and pass the Institute of World Affairs on your right $^7/_{10}$ mile farther on.

11. Bear right at fork and immediately turn right at end. Go $^4/_{10}$ mile to Hammertown Road (unmarked) on left. There's a spectacular view of the Mount Washington Range on your left as you approach the intersection.

12. Turn left on Hammertown Road and go $^9/_{10}$ mile to end (Route 41).

13. Turn right on Route 41 and go $8^3/_{10}$ miles to end (Route 23).

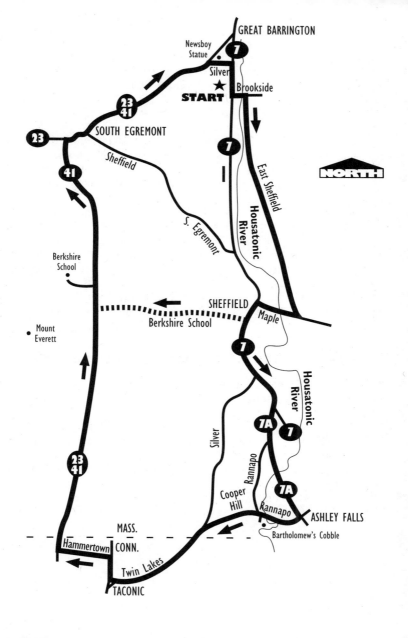

Most of this long stretch, which hugs the base of the Mount Washington Range on the left, is gently rolling. You'll pass the Option Institute and Fellowship after 4/10 mile at the Massachusetts state line. About 2½ miles farther on you'll see the elegant, red-brick Stagecoach Hill Inn on your left. The Berkshire School is on the left, set back a half mile from the road, about 2 miles beyond the inn. Mill Pond is on your left at the end.

14. Turn right on Route 23 (also Route 41 North). Go ½ mile to fork in the center of South Egremont (Sheffield Road bears right; Routes 23 and 41 bear left). You'll pass a country store and restaurant on the right.

15. Bear left on Routes 23 and 41. Go 2 9/10 miles to Newsboy Monument Lane, which bears right.

Just after you bear left, a small road turns sharply right. If you look down this road, the first building on the left looks like a small church. It is the town library, built in 1830 as a private school.

16. Bear right on Newsboy Monument Lane and go 100 yards to end (Silver Street, unmarked). You'll pass the Newsboy Statue, which was cast in 1895, on your left.

17. Bear right on Silver Street and go ¼ mile to end (Route 7).

18. Turn right on Route 7 and go less than 4/10 mile to shopping center on right.

Directions for the ride: 17 miles 〰️〰️〰️

1. Follow directions for the long ride through number 5.

2. Turn right on Berkshire School Road and go 2 7/10 miles to end (Route 41).

The road is flat and mostly wooded. You'll pass a little dam and Fawn Lake (a small pond) on your left after 2 miles. Mount Everett looms in front of you at the end.

3. Turn right on Route 41 and go 3 7/10 miles to end (Route 23). You'll pass the Berkshire School, set back half a mile from the road on your left, after 4/10 mile. Mill Pond is on your left at the end.

4. Follow directions for the long ride from number 14 to the end.

Chapter 2:
The Hill Towns

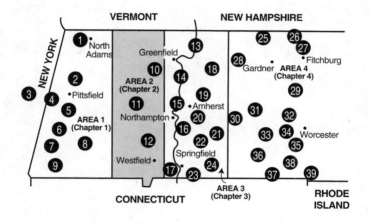

The numbers on this map refer to rides in this book.

Bridge of Flowers, Shelburne Falls

Shelburne Falls–Conway– Ashfield–Buckland

Number of miles: 26
Terrain: Rolling, with one long, steady climb and a steep, half-mile hill.
Food: Country stores in Conway and Ashfield. Snack bar in Ashfield. Restaurants at end.
Start: Municipal parking lot on Water Street in Shelburne Falls, just north of Bridge Street.
How to get there: Shelburne Falls is about 10 miles west of Greenfield and just south of Route 2. From the east, turn left off Route 2 onto Route 2A West and go about ½ mile into Shelburne Falls. Turn right on Water Street immediately before bridge, and the parking lot is just ahead on the right. From the west, turn right off Route 2 onto Route 2A East and go ⁷⁄₁₀ mile to bridge on left. Cross the bridge and immediately turn left on Water Street. The parking lot is just ahead on the right.

This ride makes a circuit of four unspoiled small towns southwest of Greenfield. Far from any metropolitan area, the landscape is very rural, with virtually no traffic except for a brief stretch on Route 2 near the end of the ride. You'll traverse a harmonious mix of woods and farmland, with hills rising in the distance across the fields.

The ride starts from Shelburne Falls, an attractive town with galleries and craft shops gracing the handsome brick buildings in the downtown area. The town spans both sides of the Deerfield River, although most of the activity is on the east bank. Crossing the river is the lovely Bridge of Flowers, a pedestrian bridge lined with plants and flowers on both sides. Built as a trolley bridge in 1908, it carried trolleys until 1928. A small trolley museum stands at the east end of the bridge, across the street from the starting point.

Another attraction in Shelburne Falls is the Glacial Potholes, a cluster of circular holes carved into the rocks along the riverbed by the swirling of water over millions of years. The larger potholes are perfect swimming holes in hot weather and a great spot to cool off after the ride.

When you leave Shelburne Falls you'll head south, following the Deerfield River, which flows far below you through a steep, narrow valley. The road diverges from the river, climbing gradually through hillside farms and then descending into Conway, a small village with a handsome domed library. You'll pass the Conway Covered Bridge, built in 1869, a short distance west of town.

From Conway, it's all uphill to Ashfield—gradually at first as you follow the South River upstream, and then steeply for the last half mile into town. Ashfield is a pristine New England village with two white churches, a fine stone library, and a graceful town hall with a bell tower. A historic landmark in town is the Zachariah Field Tavern (now a house), a long red building dating from 1792. Just past Ashfield you'll ride along Ashfield Lake, where there's a small beach and a snack bar.

From Ashfield it's all downhill to Buckland, a nearly undiscovered village tucked away on a side road off Route 112. Here you'll ride past some handsome old houses, a traditional white church, a small brick library, and a historical museum. From Buckland it's several flat miles back to Shelburne Falls through the valley of the Deerfield River; you'll follow the river closely at the end.

Directions for the ride

1. Turn left out of the parking lot on Water Street. You'll immediately come to a crossroads and stop sign (Bridge Street, unmarked). Here the ride turns right across the bridge, but to see the glacial potholes, go straight for 100 yards. Steps lead to the potholes from behind the candle shop. The center of town is to your left at the crossroads.

2. Turn right, crossing the bridge. Go 100 yards to end. The Bridge of Flowers is on the right, parallel with the automobile bridge you're crossing.

Opposite the far end of the bridge is McCusker's Market, a wonderful, old-fashioned country store. The Salmon Falls Marketplace, where you can view the works of numerous local artists and craftspeople, is on the hillside to the left of McCusker's Market.

3. Turn left at far end of bridge, and immediately bear left at fork on Conway Street, following the river on your left. Go less than $^4/_{10}$ mile to where the main road turns 90 degrees right and a dead-end road goes straight.

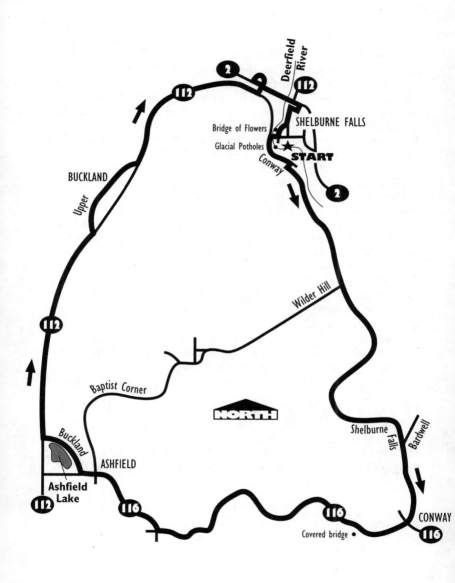

Deerfield River

2

112

112

SHELBURNE FALLS

Bridge of Flowers

Glacial Potholes

START

Conway

2

BUCKLAND

Upper

112

Wilder Hill

112

Baptist Corner

NORTH

Buckland

Shelburne Falls

Bardwell

ASHFIELD

Ashfield Lake

112

116

116

Covered bridge

116

CONWAY

4. Continue on main road for 8³/10 miles to crossroads and stop sign (Route 116), in Conway. **CAUTION:** Diagonal railroad tracks after ⁴/10 mile. You'll climb gradually as the road diverges from the river, which flows through the steep, narrow valley on your left. There's a steep descent about 2 miles before Conway. When you come to Route 116, the ride goes straight, but the center of Conway is to your left. The graceful domed library, ²/10 mile from the intersection, is worth a look.

5. Go straight at crossroads onto Route 116 North. Stay on it for 7¹/10 miles to Buckland Road on right, shortly after the center of Ashfield. You'll pass a country store shortly after you get onto Route 116, and you'll see the covered bridge on your left after ⁷/10 mile. There's a steep, half-mile climb into Ashfield.

6. Turn right on Buckland Road and go ⁸/10 mile to end (Route 112). You'll follow Ashfield Lake on your left, passing a beach and a snack bar.

7. Turn right on Route 112 and go 3 miles to Upper Street, which bears left, parallel with the main road (sign may say TO BUCKLAND CENTER). Most of this section is a steady, relaxing descent—enjoy it!

8. Bear left on this road and go 1⁴/10 miles to end (Route 112 again). You'll go through the center of Buckland after about a mile.

9. Turn left on Route 112 and go 2⁹/10 miles to fork where one road goes straight and Route 112 North curves sharply left.

10. Curve left (still Route 112) and go ²/10 mile to end (Route 2).

11. Turn left on Route 2 and go ⁶/10 mile to Route 112 North, which bears right just after the bridge over the Deerfield River.

12. Bear right on Route 112 North and go ¹/10 mile to where it turns 90 degrees right.

13. Turn right (still Route 112 North) and go ¹/10 mile to end.

14. Turn left at end, following the river on your right. Go ²/10 mile to Water Street (unmarked), which bears right.

15. Bear right on Water Street and go ¼ mile to parking lot on left. The Bridge of Flowers and trolley museum are on the right, opposite the lot.

The Heart of the Hill Towns:
Cummington–Goshen–Chesterfield–Worthington

Number of miles: 27
Terrain: Very hilly. This ride is the second toughest in the book.
Food: Country stores in the towns.
Start: Cummington Eatery (the post office is also in the building), at the junction of Route 9, Main Street, and Fairgrounds Road, in Cummington. It's on the south side of Route 9, about 20 miles west of Northampton and 25 miles east of Pittsfield.

The region midway between Pittsfield and the Connecticut River, and halfway between the Connecticut and Vermont borders, is about as rural as you can get in Massachusetts. Bicycling in this area is challenging but exciting, with long climbs balanced by thrilling descents and inspiring mountain scenery. And just when you need a rest or a bite to eat, along comes an unspoiled, traditional New England village. The ride includes a scenic highlight and also a historical one—the rugged Chesterfield Gorge and the William Cullen Bryant Homestead—both administered by the Trustees of Reservations.

The ride starts just outside Cummington, the first of the four villages on the route. You'll go through the center of town at the end of the ride. From Cummington you'll follow the fast-flowing Westfield River for about 2 miles and then endure a long, steady climb to the lovely hilltop village of Goshen. Here you'll see a handsome stone library with columns, a school with a clock tower, and the traditional white church. From Goshen, a secondary road traverses several shorter ups and downs to Chesterfield, another classic New England village with a graceful white church and pillared town hall facing each other across the road, big clapboard houses, and an inviting country store.

From Chesterfield there's a heart-stopping descent to the Westfield River—the road drops nearly 700 feet in 2 miles. You'll follow the river for about a mile to Chesterfield Gorge, a craggy canyon with the river rushing below. A steep climb brings you onto a plateau with prosperous

William Cullen Bryant Homestead, Cummington

dairy farms and views of hills on the horizon. The route then climbs more gradually to the elegant hilltop villages of Worthington Center and Worthington Corners, which are about a mile apart. Worthington Center contains an attractive white church, a town hall with columns framing the entrance, and rambling wooden houses. Worthington Corners is a classic crossroads village with an appealing country store, an old wooden library, and handsome Federal-era and Greek Revival-style houses.

Another pulse-quickening descent plunges from Worthington Corners into a narrow valley; then it's up and down (but mostly up) to the homestead of William Cullen Bryant, the eminent nineteenth-century poet and newspaper editor. The graceful, twenty-three-room mansion, with a gambrel roof and a broad porch, is set on a hillside with a sweeping view of the valley of the Westfield River and distant hills. From the Bryant Homestead it's all downhill back to the river. Just ahead, at the end of the ride, is the attractive town center of Cummington, with a brick town hall ornamented by white columns and a bell tower.

Directions for the ride

1. Turn right on Route 9. Go 6⁸⁄₁₀ miles to fork where Route 9 bears left and South Main Street (unmarked) goes straight, shortly after the village of Goshen.

At the beginning you'll cross the Westfield River and follow it closely on your right for 2 miles. The road then diverges from the river and climbs steadily for 3 miles, with a steep section about ½ mile long at the top. There's a country store on your right in Goshen.

2. Go straight on South Main Street and immediately turn right on West Street. Go 3³⁄₁₀ miles to crossroads where the main road curves sharply left. This stretch is mostly wooded and very rolling, with some steep ups and downs.

3. Stay on main road for ⁹⁄₁₀ mile to crossroads and stop sign (Route 143), in Chesterfield. You'll climb steeply for about ⁴⁄₁₀ mile near the end.

4. Turn right on Route 143 and go 2²⁄₁₀ miles to crossroads at bottom of long, steep hill (Cummington Road on right).

There's a country store on your right at the beginning as you start to go downhill. The descent is gradual at first and very steep toward the bottom. You'll cross the Westfield River again immediately before the crossroads.

5. Turn left at crossroads and go 1⁷/₁₀ mile to fork, while ascending a steep hill.

After ⁸/₁₀ mile you'll see a dirt road on your left just as you start to climb sharply. It leads 100 yards to Chesterfield Gorge, which is worth a stop. Then you'll grind up a steep, steplike hill to the fork.

6. Bear right at fork and go almost 1⁷/₁₀ miles to Radiker Road on left, at bottom of hill. You'll climb steadily for ⁴/₁₀ mile, descend briefly, and climb again steeply for ²/₁₀ mile to an open hilltop with fine views.

7. Turn left on Radiker Road and go ⁸/₁₀ mile to end (Route 112). It's all uphill, with a steep section at the beginning. Notice the graceful, Gothic-style house on your left at the end.

8. Turn right on Route 112 and go 1⁷/₁₀ miles to traffic light, in Worthington Corners. Most of this section is a very gradual climb, with a short, steep hill at the end. You'll see a small airfield on your right at the beginning and come into Worthington Center after ⁷/₁₀ mile.

9. Turn 90 degrees right at traffic light (still Route 112), passing the country store on your right. Go ⁹/₁₀ mile to where Route 143 goes straight and Route 112 turns left, at bottom of steep hill. Don't miss the intersection—you'll have to backtrack up a long, steep hill if you do.

10. Turn left on Route 112 (**CAUTION** here). Go 4¹/₁₀ miles to a crossroads where Route 112 turns 90 degrees right and the Bryant Homestead is to your left.

CAUTION: There's a steep, curving descent at the beginning. Then you'll climb steeply for ⁴/₁₀ mile, go downhill briefly, and ascend steadily for ⁹/₁₀ mile with a very steep spot near the top. At the crossroads the ride turns right, but if you turn left you'll come to the Bryant Homestead after ²/₁₀ mile. The view across the field in front of the house is magnificent.

11. Turn 90 degrees right at crossroads (still Route 112) and go 1½ miles to end (Route 9), at bottom of hill. It's all downhill! There's an excellent country store and snack bar on your right at the end.

12. Turn right on Route 9 and go ⁴/₁₀ mile to the first left (sign says TO ROUTE 116 and TO PLAINFIELD, 4 MILES). You'll follow the Westfield River on your left.

13. Turn left on this road and go ⁷/₁₀ mile to crossroads and stop sign (Route 9 again). The starting point is on the far left side of the intersection. **CAUTION:** Bumps and potholes.

You'll go through the center of Cummington and pass the town hall on your right.

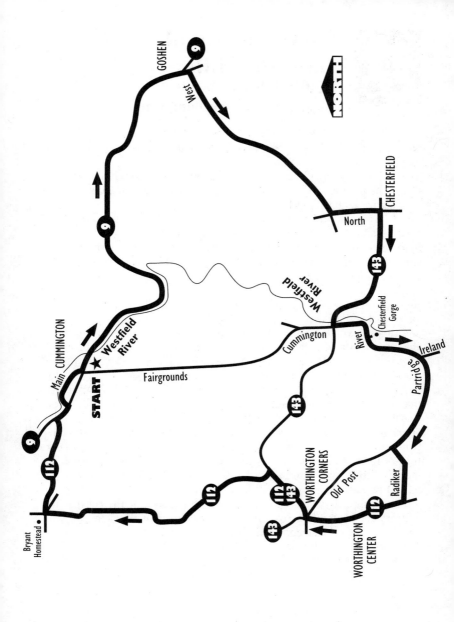

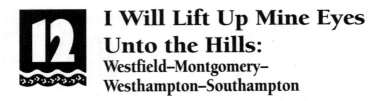

I Will Lift Up Mine Eyes
Unto the Hills:
Westfield–Montgomery–
Westhampton–Southampton

Number of miles: 36 (20 without Montgomery–Westhampton extension)
Terrain: The short ride is gently rolling, with one tough hill. The long ride is the toughest in the book, with two steep climbs more than 1 mile long, and several shorter hills.
Food: Grocery and restaurant just off the route in Southampton. Friendly's Ice Cream and Bickford's Pancakes at end.
Start: Bickford's Pancakes, Routes 10 and 202 in Westfield, next to the exit and entrance ramps for the Massachusetts Turnpike. Turn right at end of exit ramp.

Just northwest of Springfield, delightful bicycling abounds in the small valley tucked between the East Mountain–Mount Tom range on the east and rugged, wooded hill country on the west. Lying in the small watershed of the Manhan River, the valley presents a harmonious blend of broad, gently rolling farms and stands of woodland, with views of the surrounding hills across the fields.

The ride starts on the outskirts of Westfield, a small industrial city that for many years was best known as the home of Columbia bicycles. You'll immediately head into farm country as you wind along the western edge of the valley on back roads to the handsome town of Southampton, with its magnificent old white church and a brick turn-of-the-century library. From here you'll head through prosperous farmland to Pequot Pond and return to Westfield, skirting the base of East Mountain.

The long ride challenges the cyclist with a taste of the rugged hill country that extends across the western quarter of the state. As you struggle across the steep, nearly unpopulated landscape, you'll understand why the hill towns were the last part of the state to be settled. Leaving the valley, you'll climb nearly 1,000 feet to the tiny, unspoiled

80

hilltop town of Montgomery, complete with a little red schoolhouse, a traditional white church, and a wooden town hall built in 1849. From here you'll revel in a screaming downhill run to the Westfield River, only to face another long climb to get to Westhampton. This is another New England gem of a town, with a dignified white church commanding the hillside, a small, well-kept green, and a white, pillared town hall. Beyond Westhampton is a relaxing downhill run into Southampton, with spectacular views of the Mount Tom range. In Southampton you'll pick up the short ride and follow it past Pequot Pond back to Westfield.

Directions for the ride: 36 miles

1. Turn right out of the parking lot onto routes 10 and 202 and immediately ahead turn right on Arch Road. Go 1^6/10 miles to Cabot Road, which bears left just after the Agway plant on right.
2. Bear left on Cabot Road and go ^{7}/10 mile to end.
3. Turn left at end and go ^{2}/10 mile to end (merge left at stop sign).
4. Turn sharply right at end on Montgomery Road. Go 2 miles to fork (North Road bears right). Here the short ride bears right, and the long ride bears left.
5. Bear left at fork and go 7 miles to end, at stop sign (merge right on Route 112). It's a steady climb to Montgomery; you ascend 600 feet in 2 miles. Almost at the top, at the crossroads, is a little, red, one-room schoolhouse on the left, built in 1867. A mile farther on you'll pass the church and little town hall on the right. From here it's a breathtaking downhill plunge to the Westfield River. **CAUTION:** There are some sharp curves toward the bottom—don't let yourself go too fast.
6. Bear right on Route 112 and go ^{7}/10 mile to County Road, which bears right up a steep hill.
7. Bear right on County Road and go 2^4/10 miles to fork where County Road (unmarked here) turns right and Searle Road curves left, just before the church. You climb 600 feet in the first 1^2/10 miles, an average grade of 10 percent.
8. Turn right (still County Road) for ^{6}/10 mile to end, at stop sign (merge head-on into Route 66).
9. Go straight on Route 66 East for 3 miles to South Road on left, at bottom of hill (sign may say TO WESTHAMPTON, 1 MILE).

10. Turn left on South Road and go 1³/₁₀ miles to crossroads, at the church (Tob Road on left, Stage Road on right). This is the gracious village center of Westhampton. Notice the small, pillared town hall on your left at the intersection.

11. Turn right on Stage Road and go ½ mile to crossroads almost at bottom of hill (Southampton Road).

12. Turn right on Southampton Road and go 1²/₁₀ miles to crossroads and stop sign (Route 66, Main Road).

13. Cross Route 66. As soon as you cross, there's a fruit stand on your right and a magnificent view of the valley on your left. Go 2³/₁₀ miles to end (Lead Mine Road, unmarked).

14. Turn right at end and go ³/₁₀ mile to Rattle Hill Road on right.

15. Turn right on Rattle Hill Road. After ⁹/₁₀ mile the main road curves sharply left downhill at a yield sign. Continue ³/₁₀ mile to end (Pomeroy Meadow Road). Look for fine views of the Mount Tom Range to your left.

16. Turn right on Pomeroy Meadow Road and go ½ mile to end (Route 10).

17. Turn right on Route 10 and go ½ mile to East Street on left, immediately before traffic light. This is Southampton. There's a stately white church just beyond the intersection on your right.

18. Turn left on East Street, and stay on the main road for 1⁹/₁₀ miles to Middle Road on right, at top of hill.

19. Turn right on Middle Road and go 2 miles to crossroads and stop sign (Old Stage Road).

20. Cross Old Stage Road and go ½ mile to where the main road turns 90 degrees left along the shore of Pequot Pond. Immediately after the turn, an unmarked road turns right. **CAUTION:** Watch for bumps and cracks.

21. Turn right on this road and go 100 yards to crossroads (Route 202).

22. Turn left on Route 202 and go ⁷/₁₀ mile to traffic light (Old County Road on left, East Mountain Road on right). You'll pass a state-run beach on Pequot Pond on your left.

23. Turn right at crossroads onto East Mountain Road and go 2⁹/₁₀ miles to Holyoke Road on right, immediately after you go underneath the Massachusetts Turnpike and a railroad bridge.

24. Turn right on Holyoke Road and go 1⁹/₁₀ miles to end, at yield sign (merge right onto Routes 202 and 10).

25. Bear right on Routes 202 and 10. Bickford's is just ahead on left.

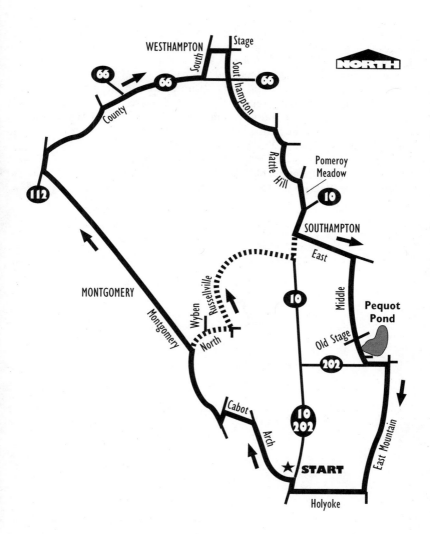

Directions for the ride: 20 miles 〰〰〰〰〰

1. Follow directions for the long ride through number 4.

2. Bear right at fork on North Road and go $^3/_{10}$ mile to an unmarked fork where Wyben Road bears slightly left and North Road bears right.

3. Bear right at fork (still North Road), and go $^8/_{10}$ mile to crossroads and stop sign (Russellville Road, unmarked).

4. Turn left at crossroads and go $3^7/_{10}$ miles to end (Route 10), in Southampton. You'll climb a tough hill.

5. Turn left on Route 10 and go $^7/_{10}$ mile to traffic light (East Street on right). Shortly before the light a handsome brick library is on your right, and at the intersection a beautiful white church is on your left.

6. Turn right on East Street, and stay on the main road for $1^9/_{10}$ miles to Middle Road on right, at top of hill.

7. Follow directions for the long ride from number 19 to the end.

Chapter 3:
The Pioneer Valley

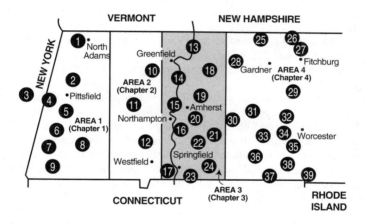

The numbers on this map refer to rides in this book.

Turners Falls–Gill– Northfield–Millers Falls

Number of miles: 29 (23 without Northfield loop)
Terrain: Rolling, with several hills.
Road surface: 1 1/10 miles of hard-packed dirt road, which can be avoided.
Food: Grocery and restaurants in Northfield. Grocery and snack bar in Millers Falls. Stores and restaurants in Turners Falls, at end.
Start: Shopping center on the main street of Turners Falls, just south of downtown.
How to get there: From Route 2, turn south at traffic light that is 3 miles east of Route 91 and 3½ miles west of the French King Bridge over the Connecticut River. Go 1 mile to the shopping center on your right.

This ride takes you exploring the Pioneer Valley just south of the Vermont and New Hampshire borders. The valley in this region is rugged and narrow, with steep hills rising almost at the water's edge, and thinly populated. Surprisingly, this remote area is home to two magnificently situated preparatory schools only 4 miles apart—Mount Hermon on the west bank of the river and Northfield on the east bank. The two schools are administered together and are collectively called the Northfield–Mount Hermon School.

The ride starts from Turners Falls, an attractive mill town right out of the nineteenth century. (For a fuller description, see the Turners Falls–Deerfield–Sunderland–Montague ride.) As you leave the town, you'll cross the Connecticut River above an impressive dam and immediately head into rugged hill country to the tiny valley village of Gill. The village center has a country store, a church, an old cemetery, a few old wooden homes, and not much else. Two miles beyond Gill, you suddenly come upon the Mount Hermon campus, impressive as any in New England, with gracious red-brick buildings spread along a broad hillside overlooking the river, and surrounded by miles of farmland and forest. Shortly after Mount Hermon, you'll cross the river again to the town of Northfield, on the east bank.

When you get to the east bank you'll pass the campus of the North-field School, another imposing group of handsome stone buildings on a hillside over the river. The town of Northfield is a New England jewel, with gracious old homes, several fine churches, and a couple of former Victorian resort hotels spaced along the main street. The elegant stone library is a New England classic. Below Northfield, you'll bike through large expanses of rich farmland extending to the water's edge. You'll pass near an underground hydroelectric power plant with a fascinating visitor's center. The facility offers boat trips on the Connecticut River from June to October. Near the end of the ride, you'll go through Millers Falls, a fascinating old mill town whose main industry is paper manufacturing. The town is also the home of Renovators Supply Company, which sells old-fashioned fittings and supplies for renovating old houses.

Directions for the ride: 29 miles

1. Turn left (north) out of the parking lot and go 9/10 mile to traffic light just after the bridge across the Connecticut River (Route 2). You will now make a small loop along the river and return to this same intersection in about a mile.

2. Turn right at traffic island immediately before Route 2, and immediately curve right on Riverview Drive, heading back toward the river. Go 6/10 mile to end (Route 2 again).

3. Turn left on Route 2 and go 3/10 mile to traffic light.

4. Turn right at light and go 6½ miles to a wide crossroads and stop sign (Route 10), shortly after the Mount Hermon campus. You'll start off with a long, steady climb, followed by a fast descent into Gill. Beyond Gill is rolling, open farmland with views of the mountains on the east bank of the river.

5. Turn right on Route 10 and go 1²/10 miles to end. Route 10 turns left here, and Route 63 South turns right. At this point the short ride turns right, and the long ride turns left.

6. Turn left and follow Route 10 for 2⁹/10 miles to Pierson Road on right. It's 4/10 mile after Route 63 turns left.

7. Turn right on Pierson Road and go ½ mile to end (Winchester Road, unmarked).

8. Turn right on Winchester Road and go 6/10 mile to Birnam Road (un-marked), which bears left at a traffic island. The gracious campus of the

Northfield School, on your right at the intersection, is worth exploring.

9. Bear left on Birnam Road and go 1½ miles to end.

10. Turn right at end and go ¼ mile to crossroads and stop sign (East Street).

11. Turn left on East Street and go ⁴⁄₁₀ mile to end.

12. Turn left at end and go less than ²⁄₁₀ mile to your first right, Captain Beers Plain Road.

13. Turn right on Captain Beers Plain Road. After ½ mile the main road bears slightly right at a traffic island. Stay on main road for ²⁄₁₀ mile to fork (Lucky Clapp Road, unmarked, bears right).

14. Bear left at fork (still Captain Beers Plain Road) and go ⁷⁄₁₀ mile to end (Route 63).

15. Turn left on Route 63 and go 1⁴⁄₁₀ miles to Pine Meadow Road on right. Here the ride turns right, but if you want to avoid the dirt road, continue straight for about 5½ miles to Millers Falls. Resume with direction number 23, heading straight uphill where Route 63 bears left onto Federal Street.

16. Turn right on Pine Meadow Road and go 2⁴⁄₁₀ miles to where the road becomes dirt. **CAUTION:** There are bad diagonal railroad tracks on this section after ½ mile.

17. Follow dirt road for ⁶⁄₁₀ mile to where it becomes paved again and continue ¹⁄₁₀ mile to crossroads. Here the ride goes straight, but if you turn right there's a lovely picnic area on the riverbank. If you'd like to visit the fascinating visitor's center of the Northeast Utilities hydroelectric plant, turn left at crossroads and go ²⁄₁₀ mile to Route 63. Turn right and immediately left, and go ¹⁄₁₀ mile to visitor's center on right. Behind the center is Northfield Mountain, an extensive area with 25 miles of trails and a lake on top. It's a popular place for cross-country skiing.

18. Go straight at crossroads, following the river on your right. After ⁴⁄₁₀ mile the road becomes dirt again. The dirt stretch is ½ mile long.

19. When the pavement resumes, continue ⁹⁄₁₀ mile to end (Route 2). You'll go underneath the high French King Bridge where Route 2 crosses the river. Just after the bridge, a small lane turns right and crosses the mouth of the Millers River over a rickety little bridge, currently blocked off to cars. It's a picturesque spot.

20. Turn right (east) on Route 2 and go ¹⁄₁₀ mile to River Road on right (it's unmarked; a sign may say TO MILLERS FALLS, AMHERST).

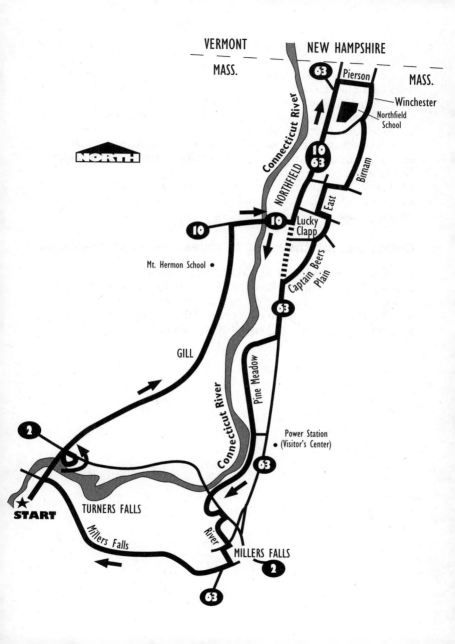

21. Turn right on River Road and go $^8/_{10}$ mile to end (Route 63), in Millers Falls.

22. Turn right on Route 63 and follow it $^4/_{10}$ mile to where Route 63 bears left onto Federal Street and another road goes straight ahead up a short, steep hill. Route 63 turns left and then right on this stretch, so follow the signs. If you go straight at the first point where Route 63 turns left, Renovators Supply is just ahead, in an old mill on the riverbank.

23. Continue straight up the hill and go $4^3/_{10}$ miles to traffic light (Avenue A) in the center of Turners Falls. **CAUTION:** Bumps and potholes at the beginning.

24. Turn left at light and go $^3/_{10}$ mile to shopping center on right, just after the traffic light. As you pull into the lot, notice the magnificent church on your left just ahead.

Directions for the ride: 23 miles

1. Follow directions for the long ride through number 5.

2. Turn right at end on Route 63 South and go $2^4/_{10}$ miles to Pine Meadow Road on right. Here the ride turns right, but see direction number 15 of the long ride if you want to avoid the dirt road.

3. Follow directions for the long ride from number 16 to the end.

Turners Falls–Deerfield–Sunderland–Montague

Number of miles: 24
Terrain: Gently rolling, with a couple of short hills. The optional climb to the Poet's Seat is moderately difficult; the optional climb up South Sugarloaf Mountain is very difficult.
Food: Groceries or restaurants in the towns.
Start: Shopping center on the main street of Turners Falls, just south of downtown. From Route 2, turn south at a traffic light that is 3 miles east of Route 91 and 3½ miles west of the French King Bridge over the Connecticut River. Go 1 mile to the shopping center on your right.

This ride has us explore a beautiful segment of the Pioneer Valley, where it is narrowed by hills rising close beside the riverbank. South of the bridge between Deerfield and Sunderland, the valley is generally wide and filled with broad tobacco farms, but as you head north of the bridge, it becomes progressively narrower all the way to the Vermont–New Hampshire line. The ride has a historical highlight: Old Deerfield, a restored community of gracious homes and inns dating from the eighteenth and early nineteenth centuries.

You start from Turners Falls, an attractive mill town with a compact business section of ornate brick Victorian buildings lining the unusually wide main street. On the cross streets are brick row houses that seem transplanted from an English industrial city. A magnificent brick church on a hillside stands proudly over the town. Just outside of town you cross the Connecticut River and enter the valley of the Deerfield River, a major tributary. You can detour one mile to the Poet's Seat, a ledge perched 350 feet above the river, offering a fine view of Greenfield, the larger twin city of Turners Falls, and the Connecticut River. A short run brings you to Historic Deerfield, a wonderful example of how an early community can be restored to its original grandeur. It's not as well known as Old Sturbridge Village, but it is equally fascinating. You can visit the houses singly or in various combinations. In the center of the village is the elegant Deerfield Inn; a handsome brick church; a spacious

91

green; and the large, gracious campus of Deerfield Academy, a prestigious preparatory school. Also in the village is the Memorial Hall Museum, which houses a collection of artifacts and relics spanning the long history of the community.

From Old Deerfield you'll follow the gently rolling valley of the Deerfield River, with soft, green hills in the distance, and then traverse a small ridge back to the Connecticut River. For a real workout you can tackle the steep climb up South Sugarloaf Mountain, where one of the finest views in the state—the entire sweep of the Pioneer Valley all the way down to Springfield—unfolds before you. You cross the river into the graceful rural town of Sunderland and pass beneath the spreading branches of the largest sycamore tree in New England. From here you'll parallel the river on the east bank along back roads through rich farmland, and pass a splendid waterfall en route.

Directions for the ride 〜〜〜〜〜〜〜〜〜

1. Turn right out of the parking lot and go 2 miles to fork, immediately after the bridge over the Connecticut River. As you leave the lot, notice the handsome church on your left. At the fork the ride bears left, but if you'd like to visit the Poet's Seat, which is 1²/₁₀ miles off the route, bear right at the fork onto Mountain Road. Go ⁸/₁₀ mile to a narrow lane that bears right at top of hill, and bear right ⁴/₁₀ mile to lookout tower. **CAUTION:** The lane leading down from the tower is very bumpy.
2. Bear left at fork and go 1 mile to a large traffic island where Routes 5 and 10 turn left. (Routes 5 and 10 also go straight at this intersection.)
3. Turn left on Routes 5 and 10. Go 1³/₁₀ miles to your first right (sign says HISTORIC DEERFIELD).
4. Turn right into Historic Deerfield. After ¹/₁₀ mile, the main road curves 90 degrees to the left. Continue on the main road ⁹/₁₀ mile to a grassy traffic island where Mill Village Road bears right and another road turns left.
5. Bear right on Mill Village Road and go 3³/₁₀ miles to crossroads and stop sign (Routes 5 and 10). Mill Village Road is a lovely lane through prosperous, broad farms, with a run along the Deerfield River. As you approach Routes 5 and 10, the two hump-shaped mountains in front of you are North Sugarloaf Mountain, elevation 791 feet, and South Sugarloaf Mountain, elevation 652 feet.

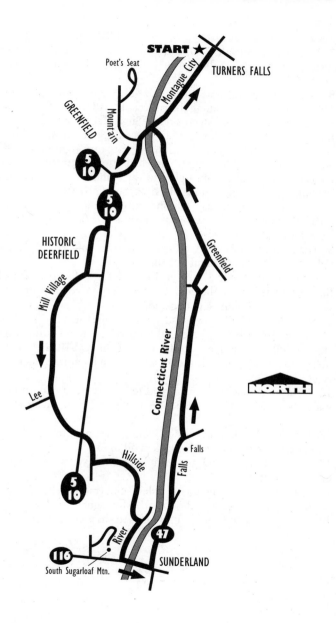

START

Poet's Seat

TURNERS FALLS

Montague City

GREENFIELD

Mountain

5
10

5
10

HISTORIC
DEERFIELD

Greenfield

Mill Village

Connecticut River

NORTH

Lee

• Falls

Hillside

Falls

5
10

47

116

River

SUNDERLAND

South Sugarloaf Mtn.

6. Cross Routes 5 and 10. Go $^7/_{10}$ mile to Hillside Road on left.

7. Turn left on Hillside Road and go $1^7/_{10}$ miles to end, at bottom of hill. A moderate climb is followed by a relaxing downhill run to the valley floor.

8. Turn right at end onto River and go $1^4/_{10}$ miles to end (Route 116). This is a beautiful run along the riverbank, with broad farms on the right ending abruptly at the steep side of Sugarloaf Mountain. At Route 116 the ride turns left, but if you'd like to tackle South Sugarloaf, the summit is $1^2/_{10}$ miles off the route. To get to the top, turn right on Route 116 and go $^4/_{10}$ mile to your first right, Sugarloaf Street. Turn right and then immediately turn right again uphill to the summit. You climb 450 feet in $^8/_{10}$ mile, for an average grade of 11 percent. **CAUTION:** On the return trip it's essential to take it easy. On one extremely steep pitch, at the hairpin turn, you should walk your bike—most bicycle brakes simply are not designed for these conditions.

9. Turn left on Route 116, crossing the river, and go $^4/_{10}$ mile to traffic light (Route 47) in the center of Sunderland.

10. Turn left on Route 47 and go $1^4/_{10}$ miles to Falls Road, a smaller road that bears left. Notice the enormous sycamore tree on your left after $^1/_{10}$ mile; it's the largest in New England.

11. Bear left on Falls Road and go $1^8/_{10}$ miles to fork just beyond the Montague town line, where Old Sunderland Road (unmarked) bears right uphill and the main road goes straight. **CAUTION:** Watch for potholes. Just before the fork there's a beauty of a natural waterfall on your right.

12. Continue straight on main road for $2^7/_{10}$ miles to South Ferry Road, which bears left at traffic island. It's just after North Taylor Hill Road on your right.

13. Bear left on South Ferry Road and go $^2/_{10}$ mile to end. You'll cross a small bridge that is currently blocked off to cars.

14. Turn left at end and go $^1/_{10}$ mile to fork (Wills Ferry Road, a dead end, bears left).

15. Bear right at fork and go $^6/_{10}$ mile to end (merge left).

16. Bear left and go $2^9/_{10}$ miles to end (Montague City Road).

17. Turn right at end and go $1^8/_{10}$ miles to shopping center on left.

Tobacco Road:
Northampton–Hatfield–Sunderland–Hadley

Number of miles: 28
Terrain: Flat. The optional climb up South Sugarloaf Mountain is very difficult.
Food: Grocery and snack bar in Sunderland. Stores and restaurants in Northampton, at end.
Start: Route 9 in Northampton opposite Smith College. Park at side of road or on a side street. If you're coming from the south on Route 91, get off at the Route 5 exit. Go north on Route 5 for 1 mile to Route 9. Turn left on Route 9 and go ½ mile to Smith College.

The heart of the Pioneer Valley, midway between the Connecticut and Vermont–New Hampshire borders, is the prime tobacco-growing region of Massachusetts. The valley here is broad and flat, with long, weathered tobacco sheds standing guard over the wide, sweeping fields, and with mountains rising in the distance.

Northampton, a city of 30,000, is one of the most attractive communities for its size in New England. In the downtown area, the unusually wide main street is lined with gracious, ornate buildings from the nineteenth century: churches, the county courthouse, city hall, the Forbes Library, old commercial buildings, and many others. It's worth visiting the downtown area on foot after the ride. Adjacent to downtown is Smith College, largest of the "Seven Sisters" schools, with 2,500 students. The tree-shaded campus mixes gracious buildings in many architectural styles. Behind the campus the Mill River flows over a beautiful little dam with a footbridge just below it.

From Northampton you'll head into tobacco country to Hatfield, among the finest of the Pioneer Valley towns, graced by a stately white church built in 1849, a handsome brick library, and old wooden homes. Many of the homes have plaques stating when they were built. Some go back to the 1700s. From Hatfield you'll continue along the Connecticut River to Sunderland, another gracious New England town. For a real challenge, you can climb South Sugarloaf Mountain and gaze in wonder at a spectacular vista with few equals in the state as the broad sweep of the Pioneer Valley unfolds for miles before you.

From Sunderland you'll parallel the river through extensive tobacco farms to the tiny village of North Hadley, with two old churches and a country store. Just ahead is the Porter-Phelps-Huntington House, an outstanding eighteenth-century residence elaborately furnished by six generations of a prominent family. A little farther on you'll ride alongside the river into Hadley, where you'll pass gracious old houses framing a long, slender green. Just beyond Hadley, you'll cross the river back into Northampton and go through the center of town at the end.

Directions for the ride

1. Head west on Route 9 and go $1^3/10$ miles to North Elm Street, which bears right at traffic light. It's immediately before Cooley-Dickinson Hospital on left.

2. Bear right on North Elm Street and go $3/10$ mile to crossroads (Hatfield Street). You'll cross the Northampton Bikeway immediately before the crossroads. To your left, the bikeway (formerly a railway) runs $1^6/10$ miles to Look Memorial Park, an unusually attractive city park. (Turn left at end of bikeway onto Bridge Road, and immediately cross Route 9 into park.). To your right, the bikeway runs 1 mile to State Street, about $7/10$ mile north of downtown Northampton.

3. Turn right at crossroads and go $3/10$ mile to end (Bridge Road).

4. Turn right on Bridge Road and then immediately left on Hatfield Street. Go $6/10$ mile to end, at stop sign (merge left on Routes 5 and 10).

5. Bear left on Routes 5 and 10. Go $1^1/10$ miles to a road on your right that crosses Interstate 91 (signs may say TO HATFIELD and I–91 NORTH).

6. Turn right on this road and go $9^2/10$ miles to fork where Sugarloaf Extension bears left and River Road bears right. Beyond Hatfield you'll see the distinctive hump of South Sugarloaf Mountain across the tobacco farms. The mountain rises in front of you at the fork.

7. Bear slightly right at fork and go $4/10$ mile to end (Route 116). Here the ride turns right, but for a real challenge you can climb South Sugarloaf. Turn left on 116 and go $3/10$ mile to your first right, Sugarloaf Street. Turn right and immediately turn right again uphill. It's $8/10$ mile to the summit, and you climb 450 feet, for an average grade of 11 percent. The

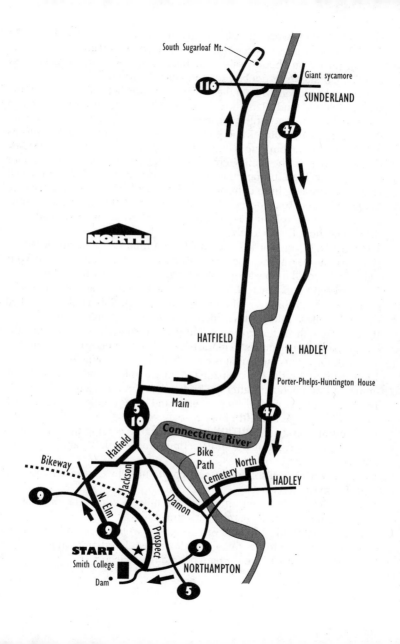

South Sugarloaf Mt.

116

Giant sycamore

SUNDERLAND

47

NORTH

HATFIELD

N. HADLEY

Porter-Phelps-Huntington House

Main

5
10

47

Hatfield

Connecticut River

Bike
Path

North

Bikeway

Jackson

Cemetery

HADLEY

9

N. Elm

Damon

9

START

Prospect

Smith College

Dam

9

NORTHAMPTON

5

view is absolutely worth the climb, even if you walk your bike. **CAUTION:** There is one extremely steep pitch as you're going down, just before the hairpin turn. You should walk your bike on this section, because even good bike brakes may not be enough to handle the gradient.

8. Turn right on Route 116 and go ½ mile to traffic light (Route 47), in the center of Sunderland. Here the ride turns right, but if you turn left and go ¹⁄₁₀ mile you'll see the largest sycamore tree in New England on your left.

9. Turn right on Route 47 and go 9 miles to North Lane on right, just as you come into the built-up section of Hadley. It's shortly after the Hadley Health Center (in the Hadley Professional Building) on right. After about 6½ miles you'll go through the tiny village of North Hadley. Here you'll pass a picturesque little dam on your left, just beyond the point where Mount Warner Road bears left. A mile beyond the dam, the Porter-Phelps-Huntington House is on your right. Shortly after, the road hugs the Connecticut River closely.

10. Turn right on North Lane and go ⁷⁄₁₀ mile to Cemetery Road on right. At the beginning, the river is behind the embankment on your right. Then you'll follow a long, slender green framed by fine homes.

11. Turn right on Cemetery Road. After ⁷⁄₁₀ mile the main road turns 90 degrees left. Continue ¼ mile to the Norwottuck Rail Trail (also called the Five-College Bike Path), which crosses the road immediately before the end. Here the ride turns right, but if you turn left you may follow the bicycle path about 8 miles to its eastern end, at Station Road in Amherst. The path follows a course that is roughly parallel to Route 9.

12. Turn right on the bicycle path and go ⁶⁄₁₀ mile to end (Damon Road, unmarked), immediately after the bridge over the Connecticut River.

13. Turn right at end of bicycle path and go ⁹⁄₁₀ mile to traffic light (Routes 5 and 10). **CAUTION:** Busy road.

14. Continue straight. **CAUTION:** A lot of traffic coming up behind you will be turning right at the intersection. Go ¼ mile to another traffic light (Jackson Street on left).

15. Turn left on Jackson Street and go ⁶⁄₁₀ mile to crossroads and stop sign (Prospect Street).

16. Turn left on Prospect Street. Go ⁸⁄₁₀ mile to where the main street curves right and a smaller street goes straight.

17. Curve right (still Prospect Street) and go ²⁄₁₀ mile to end (Route 9). Smith College is in front of you, and downtown Northampton is ⁴⁄₁₀ mile to your left. Be sure to see the dam behind the college.

The Dinosaur Ride:
Hadley–Granby–South Hadley

Number of miles: 26 (10 without South Hadley–Granby extension)
Terrain: Gently rolling, with two tough hills. The optional climb up Mount Holyoke is very challenging.
Food: Burger King at end. Groceries and restaurants in South Hadley (long ride).
Start: Mountain Farms Mall, Route 9, Hadley. It's 4 miles east of Route 91 and 2 miles west of the center of Amherst.

On this ride you explore the countryside surrounding the Holyoke Range, a prominent feature of the Pioneer Valley. The mountains lie on an east–west axis 6 miles long, averaging 800 to 900 feet high. The highest point, Mount Norwottock, has an elevation of 1,106 feet. The range is broken in the center by a steep defile known as the Notch. A road leads to the summit of Mount Holyoke, the westernmost peak, which provides a magnificent view of the valley's broad sweep and the silvery ribbon of the Connecticut River curving through it for miles.

The ride starts midway between Hadley and Amherst and immediately heads across broad farms with dramatic views of the Holyoke Range in the background. You'll pass the striking modern campus of Hampshire College. Just ahead, you'll ascend into the Notch, a steady half-mile climb, and enjoy the run down the other side. At the top of the Notch is Holyoke Range State Park, which includes a network of hiking trails and a visitor's center. Shortly after the Notch you'll come to Nash Dino Land, a rocky ledge that preserves dinosaur footprints. Just ahead is a true beauty spot of this state: the Aldrich Mill, a weathered wooden building dating from the 1830s, across the road from a picturesque dam.

From here you have a short ride to Granby, a New England gem of a town, with a large green framed by the traditional white church, Victorian town hall, and stately wooden homes. You'll now proceed to South Hadley, another gracious old town. Its centerpiece is the magnificent campus of Mount Holyoke College, the oldest women's college in the country, founded in 1837. The extensive campus, in part designed by

Frederick Law Olmsted, has two ponds, a delightful little dam, and a wealth of impressive stone and brick Gothic-style buildings.

From South Hadley you'll parallel the Connecticut River to Hadley, passing Skinner State Park, in which is the summit of Mount Holyoke. The optional climb is grueling, but the view will make it worth your while. The center of Hadley is another New England jewel, with a handsome old town hall, traditional white church, and fine old homes. The Hadley Farm Museum, in the center of town, displays early farm implements and other artifacts. A little farther on you can visit the Porter-Phelps-Huntington House, among the finest eighteenth-century houses in the state. Built in 1752, it holds an impressive collection of furnishings owned by six generations of one family.

Directions for the ride: 26 miles

1. Turn right (south) out of the east side of the parking lot onto South Maple Street and go ⁴/₁₀ mile to a crossroads and stop sign (Mill Valley Road).
2. Go straight at crossroads 1⁹/₁₀ miles to end (Bay Road). The Holyoke Range looms in front of you. At the end the short ride turns right and the long ride turns left.
3. Turn left on Bay Road and go 1¹/₁₀ miles to end (Route 116). Hampshire College, set back out of sight from the road, is on your left just before the end.
4. Turn right on Route 116 and go 2⁹/₁₀ miles to Aldrich Street, which turns sharply left (a sign may say NASH DINO LAND). It's a steady half-mile climb to the top of the Notch, where you'll pass Holyoke Range State Park on your left.
5. Turn sharply left on Aldrich Street and go ⁷/₁₀ mile to fork where one road bears right and the other goes straight. You'll pass Nash Dino Land on your left and, just ahead, the Aldrich Mill on your right. Opposite the mill is a fine dam.
6. Go straight at fork (don't bear right) and go ²/₁₀ mile to end. The millpond is on your left.
7. Turn right at end and go ¹/₁₀ mile to small crossroads (Aldrich Street on right).
8. Turn left at crossroads and go ⁷/₁₀ mile to crossroads and stop sign (Easton Street).

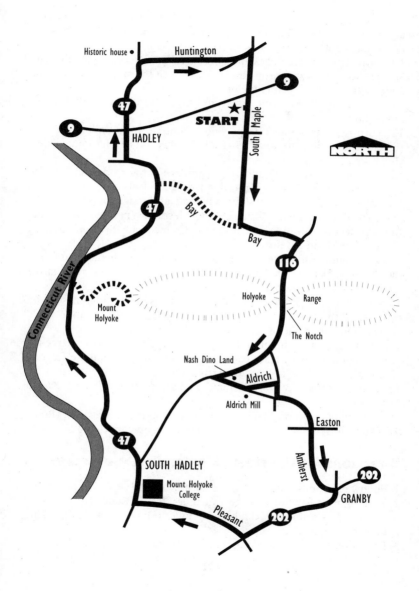

9. Cross Easton Street and go 1³/₁₀ miles to end (Route 202), in the center of Granby. The wooden Victorian town hall is across Route 202 a little to your right.

10. Turn right on Route 202 and go 1⁷/₁₀ miles to traffic light (Pleasant Street). Just after you get on Route 202, notice the splendid church on your right and the graceful little library on your left.

11. Turn right on Pleasant Street and go 1⁸/₁₀ miles to end (College Street, Route 116).

12. Turn right on Route 116, passing Mount Holyoke College on your right, and go ½ mile to Route 47 (Hadley Street) on left. It's immediately after a small green on your left.

13. Turn left on Route 47 and go 7¹/₁₀ miles to crossroads and blinking light where Route 47 turns right. If you'd like to tackle Mount Holyoke, turn right after 3½ miles on Mountain Road, at the sign for Skinner State Park. You'll have a steady 2-mile climb with some very steep pitches and gain 700 feet of elevation. You'll see the Connecticut River on your left shortly after Mountain Road.

14. Turn right (still Route 47) and go ½ mile to traffic light (Route 9) in the center of Hadley. The Hadley Farm Museum is on your right at the intersection behind the town hall.

15. Continue straight on Route 47 for 1⁷/₁₀ miles to Huntington Road on right. Here the ride turns right, but if you go straight ³/₁₀ mile you'll come to the Porter-Phelps-Huntington House on your left.

16. Turn right on Huntington Road and go 1⁷/₁₀ miles to end (merge left at stop sign into Rocky Hill Road). After you crest the hill, there's a good view of the University of Massachusetts campus.

17. Bear left on Rocky Hill Road and go ¹/₁₀ mile to traffic light (North Maple Street).

18. Turn right on North Maple Street and go 1 mile to traffic light (Route 9). The mall is on the far side of the intersection on your right.

Directions for the ride: 10 miles

1. Follow directions number 1 and 2 for the long ride.

2. Turn right on Bay Road and go 1⁷/₁₀ miles to end (Route 47).

3. Turn right on Route 47 and go ⁶/₁₀ mile to crossroads and blinking light where Route 47 turns right.

4. Follow directions for the long ride from number 14 to the end.

Agawam–Southwick–
Suffield, Connecticut

Number of miles: 30 (20 without Southwick loop)
Terrain: Gently rolling, with a few short hills.
Food: Many stores and restaurants in Agawam. Stores and restaurants just off the route in Southwick (long ride).
Start: McDonald's, Southgate Plaza, Route 75, Agawam, 1 mile south of Route 57.

This ride takes you exploring the prosperous farm country on the west bank of the Connecticut River, straddling the Massachusetts-Connecticut border just southwest of Springfield. As you head farther west, you get into tobacco country, with long, weathered tobacco sheds silhouetted against broad, flat, open fields.

The ride starts in Agawam, a middle-class suburb of Springfield, best known for Riverside Park, largest amusement park in New England. As you head west, the countryside quickly becomes rural rather than suburban. Suffield, Connecticut, is a town of extensive, gently rolling farms with some fine homes. Although close to Springfield, it has not become suburban, and, we can hope, it will remain that way. From Suffield you'll cross back into Agawam, go past Riverside Park with its convoluted roller-coaster, and enjoy a 2-mile run right along the Connecticut River.

The longer ride heads farther west into tobacco country and to Southwick, which you've probably noticed on maps because the town dips several miles below the otherwise straight border between Massachusetts and Connecticut. The jog stems from a boundary dispute that Massachusetts won in 1642. You'll go across the Congomond Lakes, a chain of three ponds separated by narrow necks of land. In the center of town, just off the route, is a handsome church built in 1824 and the Southwick Inn, an old-fashioned restaurant in an early wooden building

Directions for the ride: 30 miles

1. Turn left out of north side of parking lot onto Silver Street. Go $^7/_{10}$ mile to Garden Street on right.

2. Turn right on Garden Street and go $1^1/_{10}$ miles to where an unmarked road turns right and the main road bears left, becoming Poplar Street (unmarked).

3. Bear left on main road and go $^4/_{10}$ mile to end (Shoemaker Lane).

4. Turn right at end and go $^3/_{10}$ mile to traffic light (South Westfield Street, Route 187).

5. Turn left on Route 187 and go $1^6/_{10}$ miles to crossroads (Barry Street).

6. Turn right on Barry Street and go $^8/_{10}$ mile to crossroads and stop sign (South-West Street, unmarked). **CAUTION:** Watch for bumps and potholes.

7. Go straight at crossroads $^7/_{10}$ mile to a wide fork (North Stone Street bears left, Rising Corner Road bears right). Here the short ride bears left, and the long ride bears right.

8. Bear right at fork and go $^3/_{10}$ mile to end, at top of little hill.

9. Turn left at end and go $1^3/_{10}$ miles to a road on your right, just before a stop sign. This is a splendid run past broad farms and weathered wooden tobacco sheds.

10. Turn right on this road; and just ahead go straight at stop sign onto Route 168. Go $2^6/_{10}$ miles to Sheep Pasture Road on right, about $^1/_2$ mile after you pass between two ponds and just as you start to climb a short hill. The two ponds are part of the Congomond Lakes chain—South Pond is on your left and Middle Pond is on your right.

11. Turn right on Sheep Pasture Road and go $1^9/_{10}$ miles to end (Point Grove Road).

12. Turn left at end and go $^1/_2$ mile to end (Depot Street, unmarked). Here the ride turns right, but if you turn left and go $^2/_{10}$ mile you'll come to the center of Southwick. The Southwick Inn is a good place for a bite.

13. Turn right on Depot Street and go $^3/_{10}$ mile to fork where Powdermill Road bears left and South Longyard Road (unmarked) bears right.

14. Bear right on South Longyard Road and go $2^8/_{10}$ miles to fork where Rising Corner Road (unmarked) bears left down a sharp hill at a traffic island. This is a beautiful run through tobacco fields.

15. Bear left downhill at fork and go $^3/_{10}$ mile to another fork (North

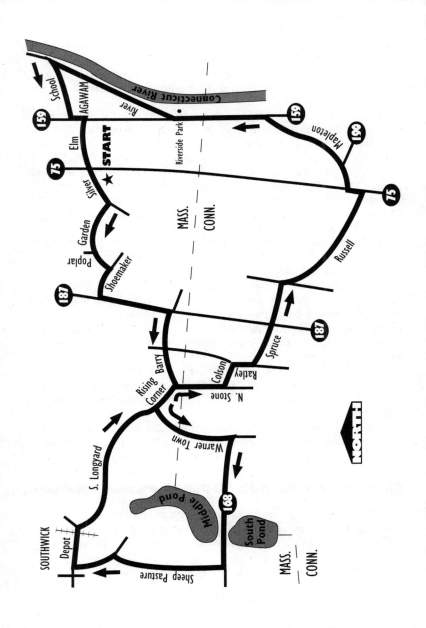

Stone Street bears right). Yes, you were here before; you've just finished the western loop and are now rejoining the short ride.

16. Bear right at fork and go $^6/_{10}$ mile to Colson Street on left.

17. Turn left on Colson Street and go $^1/_2$ mile to end (Ratley Road, unmarked).

18. Turn right on Ratley Road and go less than $^2/_{10}$ mile to Spruce Street.

19. Turn left on Spruce Street and go $^7/_{10}$ mile to crossroads and stop sign (North Grand Street, Route 187).

20. Cross Route 187 and go $^9/_{10}$ mile to end, at top of short, steep hill.

21. Turn right at end and then immediately bear left at fork on Russell Avenue (unmarked). Just ahead, curve left downhill on the main road. Go $2^2/_{10}$ miles to end (Route 75).

22. Turn left on Route 75, passing fine old homes, and go $^2/_{10}$ mile to Route 190 (Mapleton Avenue) on right.

23. Turn right on Mapleton Avenue and go $^6/_{10}$ mile to fork where Route 190 (Thompsonville Road) bears right and Mapleton Avenue bears left.

24. Bear left at fork and go $1^8/_{10}$ miles to end (East Street, Route 159). Notice sweeping views of valley on right.

25. Turn left on Route 159 and go $1^8/_{10}$ miles to River Road, which bears right at traffic light. You'll pass Riverside Park on your right.

26. Bear right on River Road and go $2^3/_{10}$ miles to School Street, which turns sharply left immediately after garage on left. This is a relaxing run along the river.

27. Turn sharply left on School Street and go $1^3/_{10}$ miles to end, at traffic light (Main Street, Route 159). **CAUTION:** Watch for bumps and potholes.

28. Turn left on Main Street and go $^1/_{10}$ mile to Elm Street on right, at traffic light.

29. Turn right on Elm Street. After $^1/_2$ mile, Elm Street bears right, but continue straight on Silver Street $^4/_{10}$ mile to Route 75, at traffic light. The shopping center is on the far left side of the intersection.

Directions for the ride: 20 miles 🖜🖜🖜🖜🖜

1. Follow directions for the long ride through number 7.

2. Bear left at fork and go $^6/_{10}$ mile to Colson Street on left.

3. Follow directions for the long ride from number 17 to the end.

Orange–Wendell–Shutesbury–New Salem

Number of miles: 31

Terrain: Hilly.

Food: Country store in Wendell; it may be closed. Restaurant in New Salem.

Start: Junction of routes 122 and 2A in the center of Orange. Park where legal at side of road.

This is a tour of the remote, isolated hill country northwest of the Quabbin Reservoir. The region is sparsely populated, with rugged, wooded hills and tiny, perfectly preserved hamlets almost unchanged since the century gone by. As you bike along the narrow, twisting roads, you're nearly as likely to encounter horses and cows in the roads as cars.

The ride starts in Orange, a compact mill town on the Millers River. It is best known for its airport, which is the major center for skydiving in the state. From Orange you'll head through deep woods and small farms to the tiny hilltop hamlet of Wendell. A miniature town hall, library, fire station, church, and school cluster around the green, some in need of a little upkeep.

From Wendell you'll enjoy a relaxing downhill run to Lake Wyola, where you can take a swim before proceeding to Shutesbury, another pristine hilltop hamlet consisting of an elegant white church, a tiny post office, several rambling old homes, and not much else. From Shutesbury you'll scream downhill to the watershed of the Quabbin Reservoir and then proceed to New Salem, a marvelous museum-piece of a town, set just far enough from the main road that the only way anyone would find it would be by accident. Fronting the large green are a splendid church, an old wooden town hall, and a wonderful old schoolhouse on top of the hill. The return leg to Orange brings you along the shore of Lake Mattawa. Just off the route you can visit the Bears Den, a steep gorge with a stream cascading over the rocks.

Directions for the ride 〰〰〰〰〰〰〰〰〰〰〰

1. Head west on Route 2A and go 2⁷/₁₀ miles to crossroads (sign may point left to Wendell Center, 5 miles). **CAUTION:** Watch for potholes for the first ½ mile.

2. Turn left at crossroads onto Depot and go 4⁶/₁₀ miles to crossroads in the center of Wendell, at the top of a long, gradual hill. **CAUTION:** Bumpy railroad tracks near the beginning.

3. Go straight at the center of Wendell 1³/₁₀ miles to fork where the main road bears right and a smaller road bears slightly left. There's a country store on the left shortly after you leave Wendell.

4. Bear right, staying on the main road. After 2 miles the main road turns 90 degrees right onto Lakeview Road. Continue ⁸/₁₀ mile to Locks Pond Road on left, just after Lake Wyola.

5. Turn left on Locks Pond Road and go 4 miles to end, in the center of Shutesbury. At first there's a long hill with steep sections.

6. Turn left at end and go 1³/₁₀ miles to end (Route 202). **CAUTION:** This is a steep descent. The end comes up while you're going downhill.

7. Turn left on Route 202 and go 5 miles to crossroads and blinking light (sign may point right to New Salem Center). There's a long, steady climb.

8. Turn right at blinking light, and after 100 yards bear right uphill, at the five-way intersection. Go ³/₁₀ mile to the far end of the green in New Salem, then backtrack to Route 202.

9. Turn right on Route 202 and go 2⁸/₁₀ miles to Elm Street, which turns sharply left (sign may say TO NORTH NEW SALEM, LAKE MATTAWA). As soon as you turn onto Route 202, you'll pass a country store and a restaurant. After ½ mile, a small turnoff on your right provides a fine view. Most of this stretch is downhill.

10. Turn sharply left on Elm Street and go ⁸/₁₀ mile to crossroads (Fay Road on right; Nelson Road on left). Here the ride goes straight, but if you turn left and go ⁴/₁₀ mile you'll come to the Bears Den on your right. Watch for a small dirt turnoff on the right. A short trail leads to the gorge.

11. From the crossroads, continue straight 3⁴/₁₀ miles to end (West River Street). You'll go along Lake Mattawa on your right.

12. Turn right on West River Street and go 1½ miles to traffic light in center of Orange (Route 122).

13. Turn left on Route 122 and go ²/₁₀ mile to Route 2A.

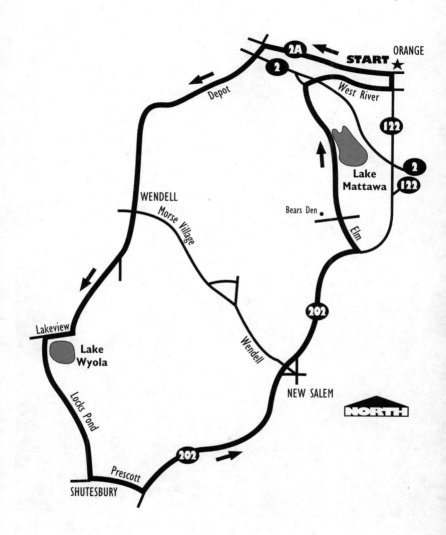

START ★ ORANGE

2A

2

Depot

West River

122

Lake Mattawa

2

122

WENDELL

Morse Village

Bears Den •

Elm

Lakeview

202

Lake Wyola

Wendell

Locks Pond

NEW SALEM

NORTH

202

Prescott

SHUTESBURY

Peace Pagoda, North Leverett

Amherst–Leverett–Shutesbury

Number of miles: 31 (21 without North Leverett–Shutesbury extension)
Terrain: Hilly.
Food: None until the end of the ride. Grocery stores and restaurants in Amherst.
Start: Newmarket Center (a shopping center), corner of University Drive and Amity Street, in Amherst. It's ⁴⁄₁₀ mile north of Route 9 and ⁶⁄₁₀ mile west of the center of town.

The wooded hills between the Connecticut River and the Quabbin Reservoir provide challenging but rewarding cycling. This is a remote, very sparsely populated area, with a few tiny pristine villages and several ponds. From Amherst you'll gain 1,000 feet in elevation as you wind your way through deep valleys up to Shutesbury; then it's all downhill back to Amherst.

Amherst (pronounced Ammerst), on top of a gradual rise at the eastern edge of the Connecticut Valley, is the largest community between Worcester and Springfield. With three colleges—University of Massachusetts, Amherst College, and Hampshire College—Amherst is the largest true "college town" in the state. During the school year, the students outnumber the residents. The three institutions are totally different in appearance and character. The massive campus of the University of Massachusetts, with more than 25,000 students, dominates the town with its sprawling, ever-growing expanse of new high-rise buildings, virtually burying the smaller number of older, traditional ones. Amherst College, in contrast, is a perfect example of the gracious, traditional New England campus. Amherst College matches the Ivy League schools in prestige and difficulty of admission requirements. Hampshire College, surrounded by farmland and orchards about 3½ miles south of town, was founded in 1970 and has a stark, ultramodern campus. Hampshire is the most unstructured and experimental of the three schools and has maintained much of the atmosphere of student activism prevalent during the late 1960s and early 1970s.

Leaving Amherst, you'll bike through a blend of farm country and woodland to the tiny villages of Leverett and North Leverett, where many residents live in harmony with nature in the spirit of the late 1960s. Leverett is the home of Leverett Crafts and Arts, one of the major centers in New England for teaching and working on traditional rural crafts. In North Leverett you can visit the Peace Pagoda, a magnificent Buddhist temple on a hilltop. It is a gleaming white dome with a gold-colored statue of the Buddha in front of it. A couple of miles ahead, you can see a coke oven dating from the 1800s and a dramatic waterfall just off the route.

Beyond North Leverett you'll climb steadily to the unspoiled hilltop village of Shutesbury, elevation 1,225 feet. It consists of a splendid church, a minuscule post office, a few rambling old homes, and that's about all. From here you finally get paid for all the work you've done up to now—it's a relaxing gradual downhill run on good roads almost all the way back to Amherst.

The short ride bypasses North Leverett and Shutesbury but comes within a mile of the latter village if you'd like to see it.

Directions for the ride: 31 miles

1. Turn right (north) out of the parking lot onto University Drive. Just ahead is a traffic light. Continue straight $8/10$ mile to end (Massachusetts Avenue). The University of Massachusetts campus is on your right.
2. Turn left on Massachusetts Avenue and go $8/10$ mile to end.
3. Turn right at end and go $1 8/10$ miles to traffic light (Route 116).
4. Cross Route 116 onto Route 63. Go $3/10$ mile to another light, where Route 63 turns left. This is North Amherst.
5. Go straight at light $4/10$ mile to State Street, which bears left downhill.
6. Bear left on State Street and go $4/10$ mile to crossroads and stop sign (Sand Hill Road, unmarked). Here the ride goes straight, but if you turn left for 50 yards you'll see an attractive dam on your right.
7. Continue straight at crossroads $6/10$ mile to end. Just beyond the crossroads, you'll pass a small pond on your left. This is Factory Hollow Pond, also called Puffers Pond, a favorite swimming hole for University of Massachusetts students.
8. Turn left at end and immediately left again on Leverett Road. (The short ride turns left at end but then continues straight ahead.) Stay on

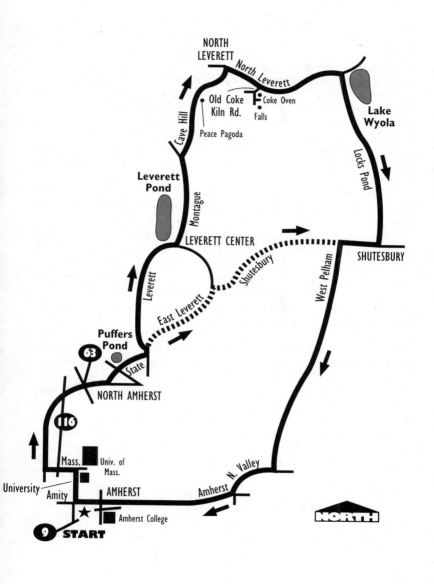

the main road 2⁶/₁₀ miles to fork where Depot Road bears left up a short, steep hill with a church on top. This is the tiny village of Leverett Center.

9. Bear left at fork and go 2 miles to Cave Hill Road, which bears right. It's just after Rattlesnake Gutter Road, a dirt road on right. You'll pass the crafts center, a long red wooden building, on your right just after you bear left up the hill.

10. Bear right on Cave Hill Road and go 2³/₁₀ miles to end (North Leverett Road). There is a long, tough climb at the beginning. After 1³/₁₀ miles, at the top, the Peace Pagoda is on the right. It's ⁴/₁₀ mile off the route on a dirt road. To see it, turn right on the entrance road for 100 yards, curve right into parking lot, and continue ³/₁₀ mile to top of hill. It's easier to walk.

When you get to the end of Cave Hill Road, you're in North Leverett, another tiny community. At the end, there's a small dam on your left and a rickety little country store, closed for years, on your right.

11. Turn right on North Leverett Road and stay on the main road for 3⁴/₁₀ miles to Locks Pond Road on right. Lake Wyola is on the far side of the intersection. If you'd like to visit the coke oven and waterfall, turn right after 1¹/₁₀ miles on Old Coke Kiln Road, a dirt road, and go ¹/₁₀ mile to fork. Bear left, staying on dirt road, and after ²/₁₀ mile you'll see the large, white conical oven, on your left. If you bear left just beyond the oven, the waterfall is 100 yards ahead on your right.

12. Turn right on Locks Pond Road and go 4 miles to end, in the center of Shutesbury (Cooleyville Road on left; Leverett Road on right). At the beginning is a long, steady climb with some steep pitches. At the end you're 1,000 feet higher than the starting point. Now the fun begins.

13. Turn right at end and go ⁹/₁₀ mile to the second left, West Pelham Road. Notice the one-room schoolhouse on the far left corner.

14. Turn left on West Pelham Road and go 4⁷/₁₀ miles to where the main road curves 90 degrees right onto North Valley Road. **CAUTION:** Potholes on the second half of this section, after the Pelham town line. After a short climb at the beginning, it's a nearly unbroken downhill run all the way to the end.

15. Curve right on North Valley Road and go 1³/₁₀ miles to crossroads and stop sign (Amherst Road, unmarked). This stretch is also all downhill.

16. Turn right at crossroads onto Amherst Road and go 2⁶/₁₀ miles to the third traffic light, in the center of Amherst, at top of hill (Pleasant

Street). Here the ride goes straight, but if you'd like to see Amherst College, turn left and go $^2/_{10}$ mile to another light (Route 9). The college is on the far side of the intersection on the left.

17. Go straight at light onto Amity Street for $^6/_{10}$ mile to shopping center on left, just before traffic light.

Directions for the ride: 21 miles

1. Follow the directions for the long ride through number 7.
2. Turn left at end. Go $2^1/_{10}$ miles to Shutesbury Road, which turns right at small traffic island at top of short hill (sign may say TO SHUTESBURY, ROUTE 202).
3. Turn right on Shutesbury Road and go $3^3/_{10}$ miles to West Pelham Road on right. After the initial steep pitch comes a long, gradual climb; you ascend from 400 to 1,100 feet. Notice the one-room schoolhouse at the intersection. Here the ride turns right, but it's worth continuing straight $^9/_{10}$ mile to visit the tiny hilltop town of Shutesbury.
4. Turn right on West Pelham Road. Go $4^7/_{10}$ miles to where the main road curves 90 degrees right onto North Valley Road. **CAUTION:** Potholes on the second half of this section, after the Pelham town line. After a short climb at the beginning, it's a nearly unbroken downhill run all the way to the end.
5. Follow the directions for the long ride from number 15 to the end.

Amherst–Belchertown

Number of miles: 27 (18 without Belchertown extension)
Terrain: Rolling, with several short, steep hills and a long, gradual climb into Belchertown on the longer ride.
Food: Grocery and restaurants in Belchertown. Burger King at end.
Start: Mountain Farms Mall, Route 9, Hadley, 2 miles west of the center of Amherst and 4 miles east of Route 91.

On this ride you explore the rolling, rural countryside on the eastern edge of the Pioneer Valley. You'll start by heading east across gently rising farmland with views of the spectacular Holyoke Range rising abruptly from the valley floor. After a few miles you'll come into South Amherst, a still-unspoiled village with a graceful white church and a large green. If you wish, you may ride the first 4⁷/₁₀ miles on the Norwottuck Rail Trail, a bicycle path built along an abandoned Boston and Maine railroad line. The bikeway is flat and smooth, with no busy road crossings. Personally, I prefer to ride on the roads, which afford better views and are less isolated from human geography.

From South Amherst you'll proceed on narrow backroads to Belchertown, among the most gracious towns in the Pioneer Valley. The magnificent town green, accented by a bandstand in the middle, is a quarter mile long and is framed by several fine churches and large, old wooden homes. Just behind the green is an old cemetery with many gravestones dating back to the 1700s. The town hosts an old-fashioned country fair each June.

For many years the town was home to the Belchertown State School, an institution for children with disabilities. The school closed in 1992 and is currently vacant. From Belchertown you'll return to the start on secondary roads through prosperous, rolling farmland with views of the Holyoke Range in the distance.

The short ride bypasses the center of Belchertown by taking a shortcut at Arcadia Lake.

Directions for the ride: 27 miles 🐛🐛🐛🐛🐛🐛

1. Turn right (south) out of the east side of the parking lot onto South Maple Street. Go ²/₁₀ mile to the Norwottuck Rail Trail, which crosses South Maple Street. Here the ride goes straight, but if you wish to try the bikeway, turn left on it and go 4⁷/₁₀ miles to end (Station Road, unmarked). **CAUTION:** The bikeway is heavily used by both cyclists and noncyclists. Keep alert for walkers, joggers, skaters, children, and dogs. Call out "Passing on your left" or "Coming through" in a clear voice when passing. Turn left at end of bikeway and go 1¹/₁₀ miles to crossroads and stop sign at top of hill (Warren Wright Road, unmarked). Resume with direction number 8.

2. Go straight for ²/₁₀ mile to crossroads and stop sign (Mill Valley Road).

3. Go straight ⁷/₁₀ mile to another crossroads (Moody Bridge Road).

4. Turn left at crossroads and go 1½ miles to crossroads and stop sign (Route 116).

5. Cross Route 116 and go ⁸/₁₀ mile to another crossroads and stop sign (Middle Street). This is South Amherst.

6. Turn left on Middle Street and go ¹/₁₀ mile to the third right (the roads come in quick succession), opposite brick school on left.

7. Turn right, and immediately go straight at crossroads onto Station Road. Go 2 miles to crossroads and stop sign at top of hill (Warren Wright Road, unmarked). **CAUTION:** The road has bumpy sections and potholes. At the beginning you'll ride through broad farms with mountains in the background.

8. Turn right at crossroads and go 1⁴/₁₀ miles to another crossroads (Orchard Street). **CAUTION:** Diagonal railroad tracks while going downhill—walk your bike across them.

9. Turn left on Orchard Street and go 1³/₁₀ miles to end (merge right at stop sign on Federal Street, unmarked). **CAUTION:** Bumps and potholes.

10. Bear right at end and go ½ mile to fork (Metacomet Street bears right). You'll follow Arcadia Lake on your left. At the fork the short ride bears right and the long ride bears left.

11. Bear left at fork and go ⁷/₁₀ mile to end (merge right on Route 9, Amherst Road). **CAUTION:** Another set of diagonal railroad tracks.

12. Bear right on Route 9 and go 1³/₁₀ miles to traffic light (Route 202).

13. Bear right on Route 202 and go ⁷/₁₀ mile to Jackson Street on right, just before the center of Belchertown. The green is on the left.

14. Turn right on Jackson Street and go 2 miles to fork where George Hannum Road goes straight and Boardman Road bears left. **CAUTION:** Bad diagonal railroad tracks after $\frac{1}{2}$ mile, while you're going downhill. There's a great view of the Holyoke Range just after the tracks.

15. Bear left at fork and go $1\frac{1}{2}$ miles to crossroads and stop sign (Route 202, East State Street). You'll pass through broad fields bordered by a stately row of trees.

16. Turn right on Route 202 and go $\frac{7}{10}$ mile to crossroads (School Street).

17. Turn right on School Street and go $3\frac{2}{10}$ miles to end (Bay Road). Shortly after turning, you'll pass Saint Hyacinth Seminary, run by the Franciscan Fathers, on your left, and Forge Pond on your right.

18. Turn left at end on Bay Road and go $2\frac{8}{10}$ miles to Southeast Street on right. It's $\frac{1}{2}$ mile after Hulst Road on right.

19. Turn right on Southeast Street and go $1\frac{9}{10}$ miles to fork at the South Amherst green. Notice the white church, built in 1825.

20. Bear left at fork on Shays Street (unmarked), and just ahead continue straight at stop sign. Go $1\frac{1}{10}$ miles to end, at stop sign (merge right on Route 116). Look for good views of the Holyoke Range to your left.

21. Bear right on Route 116 and go $\frac{3}{10}$ mile to East Hadley Road on left, immediately after bridge. Just before the intersection, an old wooden building is on your right. It was formerly a gristmill and is now an antiques shop.

22. Turn left on East Hadley Road and go $1\frac{8}{10}$ miles to crossroads and stop sign (South Maple Street).

23. Turn right at crossroads and go $\frac{4}{10}$ mile to mall on left. You'll cross the bikeway again after $\frac{2}{10}$ mile. If you turn left, it leads $3\frac{9}{10}$ miles to its western end in Northampton.

Directions for the ride: 18 miles ～～～～～～～

1. Follow the directions for the long ride through number 10.

2. Bear right at fork onto Metacomet Street and go $\frac{9}{10}$ mile to end (Bay Road).

3. Turn right on Bay Road and go 3 miles to Southeast Street on right. It's $\frac{1}{2}$ mile after Hulst Road on right.

4. Follow the directions for the long ride from number 19 to the end.

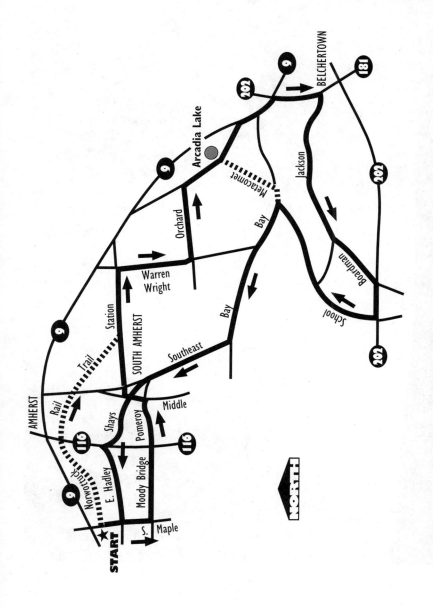

Quabbin Reservoir

The Quabbin Reservoir Ride:
Belchertown–Bondsville–Ware

Number of miles: 27
Terrain: Hilly.
Food: None on the route. Groceries and restaurants in Belchertown.
Start: Route 202, Belchertown, opposite the green. Park at side of road. If you're coming from the east, an alternate starting point is Phillip Plaza on Route 32 in Ware, 6/10 mile southwest of Route 9. Park at the southern end of the shopping center near the Crystal Springs Dairy Bar. Directions for the ride starting in Ware are at the end of the ride.

This is a tour of the southern shore of the Quabbin Reservoir, by far the largest lake in Massachusetts, with spectacular runs along Goodenough Dike and Winsor Dam, the massive, half-mile-long embankments that hold the water in its place. South of the reservoir is magnificent, rolling farmland.

You'll start from the elegant, classic New England town of Belchertown, among the finest in the Pioneer Valley. The magnificent green, highlighted by a bandstand in the middle, is a quarter of a mile long and is framed by several fine churches and large, old wooden homes. Just behind the green is an old cemetery with many gravestones dating back to the 1700s. Belchertown hosts an old-fashioned country fair in June.

From Belchertown you'll head south through rolling farmland and orchards to the little valley town of Bondsville, which straddles the Belchertown-Palmer line along the Swift River. From here you'll follow the delightful valley of the Ware River, with views of rugged hills on both sides, to the outskirts of Ware, a nineteenth-century mill town straight out of the Industrial Revolution. Ware is one of the great bargain centers for clothing and sportswear in New England; most of the mills have factory outlets. The majority of the mills are clustered in one enormous complex called the Industry Yard.

Beyond Ware comes the exciting part of the ride, as you follow the southern shore of the Quabbin Reservoir back to Belchertown. Physically, the reservoir is impressive, 15 miles long and dotted with rugged, mountainous islands rising steeply from the water like dorsal fins. The uninhabited Prescott Peninsula splits the reservoir into two unequal parts, the western arm a long, slender ribbon less than a mile wide. Access to the water is limited, because most of the shoreline consists of cliffs and steep hills rising directly from the water's edge. The Quabbin was created in 1939 and 1940 by damming the Swift River, flooding five small villages. Its waters flow 80 miles through an elaborate system of aqueducts to supply the Boston metropolitan area, passing through the Wachusett Reservoir, the state's second-largest lake, en route.

You first encounter the reservoir at the 2,000-foot-long Goodenough Dike and then climb 400 feet to the handsome stone lookout tower atop Quabbin Hill, elevation 1,025 feet. From the observation deck a spectacular view of the entire reservoir unfolds in front of you. On a clear day you can easily see Mount Monadnock, 40 miles to the north. The watershed is a breeding ground for bald eagles, and if you're very lucky you may see one glide past. From the tower it's all downhill to 125-foot-high Winsor Dam, the second-largest earth dam east of the Mississippi (the largest is Saluda Dam in South Carolina). After the spectacular run across the top of the dam, it's a short way back to Belchertown.

Directions for the ride: Belchertown start 〰️〰️

1. Head south on Route 202, following the Belchertown green on your left. Just ahead, at the end of the green, is a traffic light where Route 202 turns right and Route 181 goes straight.
2. Go straight onto Route 181 for 2$\frac{1}{10}$ miles to Cold Spring Road, a small road that bears left at top of hill. Notice the handsome stone library on your left at the beginning. There's a relaxing downhill run out of Belchertown.
3. Bear left on Cold Spring Road and go $\frac{7}{10}$ mile to fork. This is a delightful run past farms and orchards.
4. Bear right at fork onto Michael Sears and go 1$\frac{2}{10}$ miles to end (Route 181). You'll ascend onto a ridge with panoramic views.
5. Turn left on Route 181. After 1$\frac{3}{10}$ miles, Route 181 curves sharply left and a smaller road goes straight. Stay on Route 181 for $\frac{3}{10}$ mile to end. This is Bondsville.
6. Turn right at end (still Route 181) and go $\frac{2}{10}$ mile to crossroads, fac-

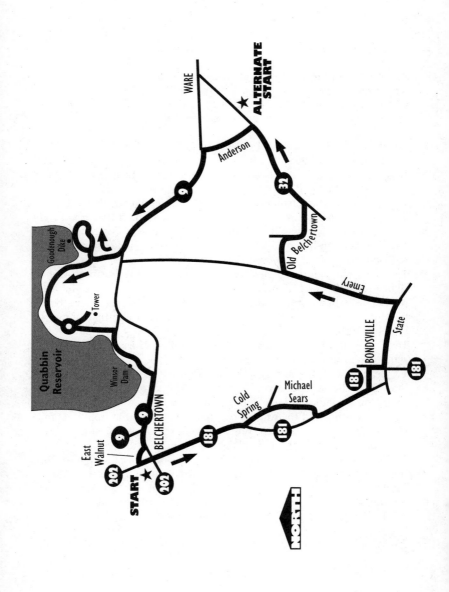

ing a church. Route 181 bears slightly right at the intersection.

7. Turn left in front of the church onto State and go 1½ miles to Emery Street on left, at bottom of steep hill after railroad tracks and immediately before bridge.

8. Turn left on Emery Street and go 2½ miles to Old Belchertown Road, which turns right down a steep hill. It's the first right after the airport. **CAUTION:** Diagonal railroad tracks after $6/10$ mile.

9. Turn right on Old Belchertown Road and go $6/10$ mile to end (merge right on Seaver Lake Road).

10. Bear right at end and go $9/10$ mile to end (Route 32).

11. Turn left on Route 32 and go $1^1/10$ miles to crossroads (Malboeuf Road on right, Anderson Road on left.) You reach the crossroads while you're going downhill.

12. Turn left on Anderson Road and go $1^2/10$ miles to end (Route 9).

13. Turn left on Route 9 and go $2^4/10$ miles to a road that bears right through a pair of stone pillars about 100 yards ahead.

14. Bear right on this road and go $8/10$ mile to fork (sign may point right to Goodenough Dike).

15. Bear right at fork. After $1/10$ mile a road bears left, but bear slightly right downhill. Go $1^6/10$ miles to a grassy traffic island where the main road curves sharply right and another road turns left. You'll pass below the dike, climb steeply to the level of the reservoir, and bike along the top of the dike.

16. Curve right on main road and go $1/10$ mile to fork (sign may point right to Winsor Dam).

17. Bear right at fork and go 2½ miles to rotary. There's a steady, mile-long hill at the end. Be sure to stop at Enfield Lookout, shortly before the rotary, for a panoramic view of the entire reservoir.

18. Go two-thirds of the way around the rotary and head uphill $3/10$ mile to summit. The view from the observation tower is magnificent.

19. From the summit, backtrack $3/10$ mile to the rotary.

20. Go almost all the way around the rotary, following the sign to Winsor Dam, and go $1^4/10$ miles to end. This is an exhilarating downhill run.

21. Turn right at end and immediately curve right on the main road. Go $1^1/10$ miles to end (Route 9), going along the top of Winsor Dam.

22. Turn right on Route 9 and go 2 miles to Route 21 (Jabish Street) on left.

23. Turn left on Route 21 and go ½ mile to East Walnut Street on right.

It's just after Eastview Drive on right.

24. Turn right on East Walnut Street and go ³/₁₀ mile to end (Route 202, North Main Street), at top of hill.

25. Turn left on Route 202. The Belchertown green is on your left.

Directions for the ride: Ware start ~~~~~~~~~~
(Start at Phillip Plaza, Route 32.)

1. Turn left (southwest) on Route 32 and go ⁹/₁₀ mile to crossroads (Malboeuf Road on left, Anderson Road on right).

2. Turn right on Anderson Road and go 1²/₁₀ miles to end (Route 9).

3. Follow directions number 13 through 24 for the ride starting in Belchertown.

4. Turn left on Route 202 and go ²/₁₀ mile to traffic light at the end of the Belchertown green. At the light Route 202 turns right and Route 181 goes straight.

5. Follow directions number 2 through 10, to Route 32.

6. Turn left on Route 32 and go 2 miles to shopping center on right. Crystal Springs Dairy Bar, in the shopping center, is a good spot for a bite.

Ludlow–Belchertown–
Three Rivers

Number of miles: 25 (17 without Belchertown–Three Rivers extension)
Terrain: Gently rolling, with two long, tough hills and one moderate hill.
Food: Grocery and restaurant in Belchertown and Three Rivers (25-mile ride).
Start: Small shopping center at 477 Center Street (Route 21), next to Friendly Ice Cream in Ludlow. It's immediately north of the entrance and exit ramps for the Massachusetts Turnpike. Turn right at end of exit ramp.

The region northeast of Springfield, consisting of rolling farmland and low, forested hills, provides relaxing bicycling on a network of lightly traveled backroads. Ludlow is an old industrial town with an enormous nineteenth-century mill complex stretching half a mile along the Chicopee River. The ride starts from the outskirts of town and immediately heads north into rolling farm country with views of the Holyoke Range rising in the background. You'll cut across a wooded ridge and climb sharply into Belchertown, a gracious hilltop town with a long green that has a bandstand in the middle. From Belchertown you'll descend into a beautiful valley with expansive, gently rolling farms and orchards. Suddenly you'll enter the small mill town of Three Rivers, where the Ware and Quaboag rivers join to form the Chicopee, which flows into the Connecticut River at Springfield. From here you'll parallel the Chicopee River to a fine old dam with a spillway 40 feet high; behind it the river is backed up into an unspoiled pond.

The short ride bypasses Three Rivers to take a more direct route back to Ludlow. You'll pass the Springfield Reservoir, part of the water supply for Springfield, and then bike through the part of Ludlow that was its center before the town became industrialized, with a distinctive church and an old cemetery.

Directions for the ride: 25 miles ~~~~~~~~~~

1. Turn left (north) out of parking lot onto Route 21 and go $^8/_{10}$ mile to Rood Street on left. There's a great fruit and vegetable stand at the intersection.

2. Turn left on Rood Street and go $^7/_{10}$ mile to Church Street on right.

3. Turn right on Church Street and go $^2/_{10}$ mile to fork where Munsing Street bears left.

4. Bear left on Munsing Street and go 1 mile to end (merge left on Lyons Street).

5. Bear left on Lyons Street and go 1$^9/_{10}$ miles to end (Carver Street, unmarked). You pass through inspiring, rolling farmland, with glimpses of the Holyoke Range in the distance. The peak with the distinctive sharp dropoff is Long Mountain.

6. Turn right on Carver Street. Go 3$^2/_{10}$ miles to Rockrimmon Road (unmarked), which turns left immediately before you start to go downhill on Granby Road. It's just after Maplecrest Drive (unmarked) and house number 176 on left. **CAUTION:** Bumpy spots and potholes.

7. Turn left on Rockrimmon Road and go $^9/_{10}$ mile to end (Route 21). Here the short ride turns right and the long ride turns left.

8. Turn left on Route 21 and go 1$^3/_{10}$ miles to end (Route 202).

9. Turn right on Route 202 and go 1 mile to traffic light in the center of Belchertown (Route 202 on left, Route 181 on right). There's a steep hill at the end. The town green and business district are to your left at the light.

10. Turn right at light on Route 181 and go $^1/_4$ mile to North Washington Street (unmarked), which bears right. A sign may say TO THREE RIVERS. Notice the handsome stone library on your left at the beginning.

11. Bear right on North Washington Street. Go 2$^1/_{10}$ miles to where North Washington Street bears right onto a smaller road (the main road becomes North Liberty Street at the intersection). **CAUTION:** This road makes an S-curve under a narrow railroad bridge; sand often builds up here.

12. Bear right on North Washington Street and go 1 mile to end.

13. Turn left at end and immediately right on South Washington Street. Go 1$^3/_{10}$ miles to crossroads (West Street). This is beautiful, open farmland.

14. Turn left at crossroads onto West Street and go $9/10$ mile to crossroads and stop sign.

15. Turn right at crossroads (South Street) and go $2\frac{1}{10}$ miles to crossroads and stop sign just after bridge (Springfield Street, unmarked). From the bridge there's a fascinating view of the Chicopee River as it flows between two old mills. At the crossroads the ride turns right, but if you turn left, stores and restaurants are just ahead in the center of Three Rivers.

16. Turn right on Springfield Street and go 5 miles to traffic light (Chapin Street). It's $6/10$ mile after you go underneath the Massachusetts Turnpike. After $2\frac{4}{10}$ miles, watch for a grassy embankment on your right, just as you start to go downhill. Behind the embankment is the dammed-up Chicopee River, a perfect spot for a picnic. As you start down the hill, you can see the dam on your right, and you'll pass an old brick pumping station on your left. At the bottom of the hill you'll cross the river itself.

17. Turn right at light on Chapin Street and go $1\frac{1}{10}$ miles to Route 21 (Center Street), at traffic light.

18. Turn left on Route 21 and go $\frac{1}{2}$ mile to shopping center on right.

Directions for the ride: 17 miles ❧❧❧❧❧❧❧❧❧

1. Follow directions for the long ride through number 7.

2. Turn right on Route 21 and go $8\frac{2}{10}$ miles to shopping center on right. You'll pass the Springfield Reservoir on your right. A mile and a half beyond the reservoir you'll go through the old center of Ludlow; the main road bears left here at a fork.

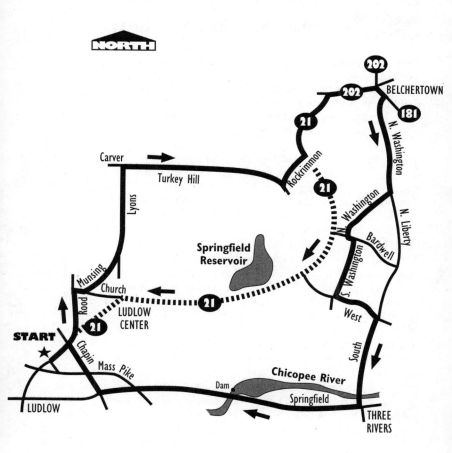

Longmeadow–
East Longmeadow–
Somers, Connecticut

Number of miles: 29 (18 without eastern hills extension, 14 with shortcut)
Terrain: Gently rolling, with one moderate hill and one tougher one. The 29-mile ride has an additional steady climb 1½ miles long.
Food: None until near the end of the ride. Better bring your own.
Start: Junction of Routes 5 and 192 (Williams Street) in Longmeadow, 2 miles south of the Route 5 exit from Route 91. Park on Route 192.

The gently rolling farmland southeast of Springfield, with views of the rugged hills several miles to the east across broad fields, provides relaxed and very scenic biking on a wealth of lightly traveled secondary roads. The ride starts from the center of Longmeadow, Springfield's most prosperous suburb. The town is well named—the green is so long it's practically a meadow. Its half-mile length makes it the longest green in the state. It is also one of the most gracious, lined on both sides with handsome old homes dating back to the 1800s and earlier; a graceful church; and two old brick schools. The Storrs Parsonage, built in 1786, and the Colton House, built in 1734, are both open by appointment.

From Longmeadow you'll head along quiet suburban streets to East Longmeadow, another pleasant residential community, best known as the home of Milton Bradley, the games company. As you head east out of town and then south across the Connecticut line, the landscape becomes more and more rural, with broad sweeps of farmland and views of the mountains in the distance. You'll go past a cluster of Connecticut state prisons, incongruously located in the midst of acres of rolling farmland.

The long ride offers a real workout by heading eastward beyond the valley into the wooded hills. You'll climb 500 feet to a plateau dotted with small farms and then enjoy the long, gradual descent back into the valley. The return to Longmeadow leads through gently rolling farmland with inspiring views of the mountains you've just conquered.

The 14-mile ride takes a more direct route from East Longmeadow back to the end and is not quite so rural.

Directions for the ride: 29 miles

1. Head east on Williams Street and go 2⁶/₁₀ miles to third traffic light (Dwight Road on left, Benton Drive on right). Shortly before the first light, Route 192 bears right onto Shaker Road, but go straight here on Williams Street.

2. Continue straight for 1³/₁₀ miles to stop sign in the center of East Longmeadow, where seven roads come together. Here the 14-mile ride turns right onto Route 186 (Prospect Street) immediately after the stop sign, and the two longer rides continue straight.

3. Continue straight, crossing Route 83 onto Pleasant Street. After ⁹/₁₀ mile, the main road curves sharply right at bottom of hill. Stay on the main road for ⁹/₁₀ mile to crossroads and blinking light (Parker Street).

4. Turn right on Parker Street and go 1⁹/₁₀ miles to stop sign and blinking light (Hampden Road).

5. Continue straight for ⁶/₁₀ mile to end. Notice the old church to your right at the intersection.

6. Turn left at end and then immediately bear left on Mill Road. (The 18-mile ride turns left at end and then bears right on the main road.) Go 1⁷/₁₀ miles to end (Somers Road).

7. Turn right on Somers Road and go 1¹/₁₀ miles to fork (Isaac Bradway Road bears left).

8. Bear left on Isaac Bradway Road and go ⁴/₁₀ mile to end (Stafford Road), at stop sign. You are now in Connecticut.

9. Bear left uphill at end. Go ⁶/₁₀ mile to fork where Root Road bears right and the main road bears slightly left. It's all uphill.

10. Bear left on main road and go 1⁹/₁₀ miles to end (Old Springfield Road on left, Mountain Road on right). Most of this section is a long, steady climb with some steep pitches. If you turn right after 1⁶/₁₀ miles at the crossroads on Camp Road, a dirt road, you'll find a little pond after ¹/₁₀ mile. It's a great spot to rest after the long climb.

11. Turn right onto Mountain Road and go 2⁴/₁₀ miles to crossroads and stop sign (Turnpike Road). This is a fine downhill run. Notice the unusual castlelike stone house on your left after 1⁶/₁₀ miles.

12. Cross Turnpike Road and go ¹/₁₀ mile to Stebbins Road, a smaller road that bears right.

13. Bear right on Stebbins Road and go 1 mile to crossroads and stop sign (Springfield Road, Route 83).

14. Turn right on Route 83 and go 1½ miles to a small crossroads (Grist Mill Terrace on right, King Road on left).

15. Turn left on King Road and stay on main road 1¹/₁₀ miles to end (Watchaug Road).

16. Turn left on Watchaug Road and go 1 mile to crossroads and stop sign (Four Bridges Road). Route 186 goes straight at the intersection. This is a magnificent run through broad farms, with the mountains in the distance.

17. Go straight at crossroads onto Route 186, bearing left as you go through the intersection. Go ½ mile to crossroads and blinking light (George Wood Road).

18. Turn right on George Wood Road and go 1³/₁₀ miles to crossroads and stop sign (Somers Road).

19. Turn right on Somers Road and go ²/₁₀ mile to end (Taylor Road, unmarked).

20. Turn right on Taylor Road and go ⁴/₁₀ mile to crossroads and stop sign (Shaker Road on left). The buildings at the top of the hill to your right are a Connecticut state prison.

21. Turn left at crossroads onto Shaker Road and go ⁸/₁₀ mile to Bacon Road on right. You'll pass another prison on the right at the beginning.

22. Turn right on Bacon Road and go ⁷/₁₀ mile to end (North Maple Street, Route 192).

23. Turn right on North Maple Street. Go ³/₁₀ mile to fork immediately after stop sign, where Brainard Road goes straight and North Maple Street (Route 192) bears right.

24. Bear right at fork and go ⁹/₁₀ mile to crossroads and blinking light (Maple Road) immediately after you cross the state line back into Longmeadow.

25. Turn left on Maple Road and go 1½ miles to end (Route 5), at traffic light.

26. Turn right on Route 5 and go 1²/₁₀ miles to Route 192. When you get to the green, there's less traffic if you take the road along the right-hand side of the green.

Directions for the ride: 18 miles ~~~~~~~~~

1. Follow directions for the 29-mile ride through number 5.

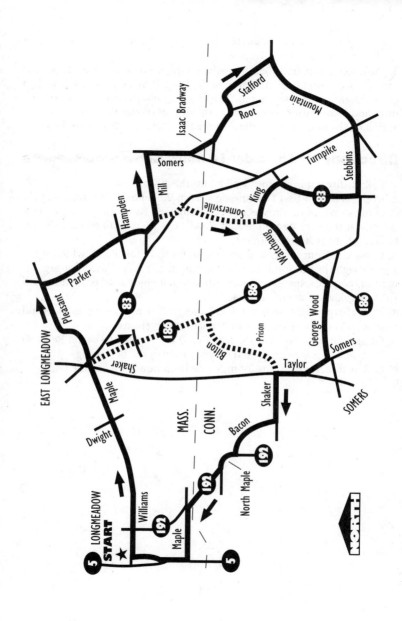

2. Turn left at end and immediately bear right at fork, staying on main road. Go $^4/_{10}$ mile to end (Route 83).

3. Turn left at end and then immediately right on Somersville Road. Go 2½ miles to crossroads and stop sign (Four Bridges Road). Route 186 goes straight at the intersection. This is a magnificent run past horse pastures and broad farms with views of the distant mountains.

4. Follow the directions for the 29-mile ride from number 17 to the end.

Directions for the ride: 14 miles

1. Follow directions number 1 and 2 for the 29-mile ride.

2. In the center of East Longmeadow, turn 90 degrees right immediately after the stop sign on Prospect Street, Route 186 (don't turn sharply right directly at the stop sign on Shaker Road). Go $^7/_{10}$ mile to crossroads and blinking light (Chestnut Street).

3. Cross Chestnut Street and go $1^7/_{10}$ miles to Bilton Road, which turns sharply right just beyond the Connecticut line. You'll climb a long, gradual hill, passing expensive homes; then you'll enjoy a relaxing downhill run with views of the mountains.

4. Turn sharply right on Bilton Road and go $2^1/_{10}$ miles to crossroads and stop sign. You'll pass several Connecticut state prisons.

5. Go straight at crossroads (Shaker Road) for $^8/_{10}$ mile to Bacon Road on right. You'll pass another prison on your right at the beginning.

6. Follow directions for the 29-mile ride from number 22 to the end.

24 Wilbraham–Monson–Hampden

Number of miles: 22 (17 without Monson extension)
Terrain: Hilly in the first half; gently rolling in the second half.
Food: Grocery and restaurant in Monson (22-mile ride). Grocery in Hampden.
Start: Small shopping center on Burt Lane and Crane Park Drive in center of Wilbraham, just east of Main Street.
How to get there: From the junction of Routes 20 and 21 in Springfield, head east on Route 20 for about 3½ miles until you see a pond on your right. Shortly after it, bear right at a traffic island and then immediately turn right on Main Street. Go 2¹/₁₀ miles to Burt Lane and Crane Park Drive on left, shortly after the Wilbraham and Monson Academy (the street sign says both names). If you're coming from the east, Main Street bears left from Route 20, 5 miles west of Route 32 North in Palmer, shortly after you go under a railroad bridge.

The rounded hills beyond the Pioneer Valley east of Springfield provide challenging but dramatic bicycling on good roads. This is an area of long climbs but equally long descents, with fine views from the tops of the ridges. The ride starts from Wilbraham, a well-to-do suburb of Springfield that lies partly in the valley and partly along the steep hills rising from its eastern edge. The town is more rural than suburban. The center of town is graced by the handsome campus of Wilbraham and Monson Academy, a prestigious preparatory school. The town is also the site of the main office of the Friendly Ice Cream Corporation, whose restaurants are in every town of any size throughout the state. You may have noticed Friendly's floral "Welcome to Wilbraham" greeting planted on a hillside as you're driving west on the Massachusetts Turnpike.

As you leave Wilbraham you'll immediately climb onto Wilbraham Mountain, the high ridge forming the eastern edge of the Pioneer Valley. It's a long ascent but the view from the top is superb. On a clear day you can see far beyond Springfield to the Berkshires. After enjoying the spectacular run along the top of the ridge, you'll head mostly downhill through a mixture of woods and rolling farmland to the quiet crossroads town of Hampden. Hampden is best known as the home of Thornton Burgess, one of America's best-known writers of animal stories. His house, built in 1742, stands next to the Laughing Brook Educational Center and Wildlife Sanctuary, run by the Massachusetts Audubon Society. In the center of town stands Academy Hall, a splendid old schoolhouse built in Greek Revival style. Leaving Hampden, you'll enjoy a smooth, fairly flat ride back to Wilbraham, passing small farms and fine older houses.

The longer ride heads farther east to the small mill town of Monson (pronounced Munson). As mill towns go, Monson is one of the most attractive in the state, with a graceful white church, a handsome Victorian stone library, and an ornate granite town hall with a clock tower, built in 1884. Leaving Monson, you wind gradually uphill through rolling, pastoral countryside. You'll be rewarded with some fine views and a smooth downhill run into Hampden.

Directions for the ride: 22 miles 🪱🪱🪱🪱🪱🪱🪱

1. At the end of Burt Lane and Crane Park Drive, turn right on Main Street and go $\frac{1}{10}$ mile to Mountain Road on right. Notice the beautiful stone church on the far corner. Just beyond the church is the impressive main building of Wilbraham and Monson Academy.
2. Turn right on Mountain Road and go $1\frac{4}{10}$ miles to end, at traffic island (Ridge Road). This is a long, steady climb.
3. Turn right on Ridge Road and go $1\frac{7}{10}$ miles to end. To your right are unsurpassed views of the Pioneer Valley across the lawns of expensive homes.
4. Turn left onto Monson and go $3\frac{1}{10}$ miles to end, at stop sign (merge left at bottom of hill). Just after you turn left there's an exciting downhill run on smooth pavement—enjoy it! At the stop sign the short ride turns sharply right and the long ride bears left.
5. Bear left at stop sign. Go $2\frac{3}{10}$ miles to the second of two stop signs a block apart, where you merge head-on into Route 32 in Monson. Immediately before the intersection there's a handsome stone church on the left. Also notice the ornate Victorian library, built in 1881, on your right at the intersection.

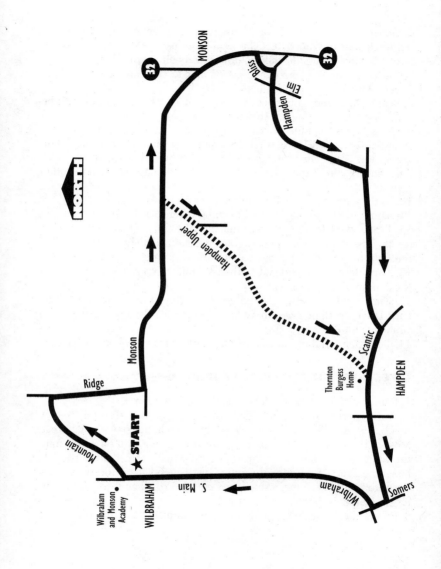

6. Go straight on Route 32 for ⁹/₁₀ mile to Bliss Street on right, just after a red-brick mill on your left. (The road is unmarked; a sign may say TO HAMPDEN.) You'll pass the tall Victorian town hall on your left.

7. Turn right on Bliss Street and go ²/₁₀ mile to end (merge right on Oak Street). There is no stop sign here.

8. Bear right at end, going between a pair of ancient, grim mills. Just beyond the mills is a diagonal crossroads (Elm Street).

9. Cross Elm Street onto Lower Hampden Road and go 5⁴/₁₀ miles to end (Scantic Road). **CAUTION:** After 2⁴/₁₀ miles the main road curves 90 degrees right while you're going down a steep hill. You'll start off with a long, steady climb; then the road descends through magnificent rolling countryside.

10. Turn right on Scantic Road and go ½ mile to stop sign.

11. Continue straight for 2 miles to end (Somers Road). At the beginning you'll pass the Laughing Brook Educational Center on the right. Thornton Burgess's home, a small gray cottage, is immediately after it. You'll go through the center of Hampden about ½ mile farther.

12. Turn right at end and go less than ²/₁₀ mile to crossroads (Wilbraham Road, unmarked, on right).

13. Turn right at crossroads and go 4⁴/₁₀ miles to Burt Lane and Crane Park Drive on right, back in Wilbraham. Notice the fine old homes as you come into the town.

14. Turn right on Burt Lane and Crane Park Drive into shopping center.

Directions for the ride: 17 miles 〰️〰️〰️

1. Follow directions for the long ride through number 4.

2. Turn sharply right at stop sign and go 6⁴/₁₀ miles to end (Somers Road). Two smaller roads bear left on this stretch, but stay on main road. Most of this section is a relaxing, gentle downgrade. After about 4 miles the road curves sharply to the right, and you'll immediately pass the Laughing Brook Educational Center. Just beyond it on the right is the Thornton Burgess Home, a small gray cottage. You'll go through the center of Hampden about ½ mile farther.

3. Follow directions for the long ride from number 12 to the end.

Chapter 4:
Central Massachusetts

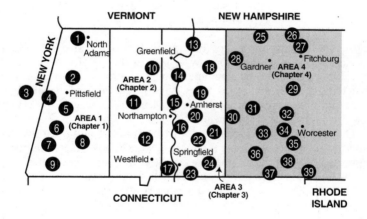

The numbers on this map refer to rides in this book.

Cathedral of the Pines Ride:
Winchendon–Rindge, New Hampshire

Number of miles: 20
Terrain: Rolling, with several moderate hills and one tough one.
Road surface: $\frac{9}{10}$ mile of very bumpy and potholed road, which can be avoided.
Food: Country store in Rindge. Groceries and Dunkin' Donuts at end.
Start: Shopping center at junction of Routes 12 and 202 in the center of Winchendon. Entrance is on Route 202.

On this ride you explore a very rural, primarily wooded area of low hills around Lake Monomonac, the largest lake in the vicinity. You'll head several miles north of the state line through the stately hilltop town of Rindge to the Cathedral of the Pines, one of New England's true beauty spots, and return to Winchendon on back roads by way of the classic New England village of Winchendon Center.

The ride starts in Winchendon, a small, compact mill town that for years was the country's prime producer of wooden toys, especially rocking horses. Most of the original toy factories have been demolished, and the few remaining mills now house diversified industries.

From Winchendon you'll head north across the New Hampshire border along narrow wooded roads to Rindge, a graceful old hilltop town with a traditional New England church and green, along with a fine red-brick Victorian library. From here you're not far from the Cathedral of the Pines, one of New England's most beautiful attractions. The Cathedral is a nondenominational chapel set in a grove of pines on top of a hill with a magnificent view of Mount Monadnock and its neighboring peaks. A tall, delicate bell tower stands at the entrance to the grove. The Cathedral was founded in 1945 by Douglas and Sybil Sloane, who lived in the farmhouse at its entrance, as a memorial to their son, a pilot who was shot down over Germany during World War II.

From the Cathedral you'll head back to Winchendon with a run along the shore of Lake Monomonac. Just before the end you'll go through the tiny hilltop village of Winchendon Center, with a beautiful old church standing proudly above a little green, and enjoy a fast downhill run back into town. The road leading to Winchendon Center is in very poor condition, but you can easily bypass the village by following Route 12.

Directions for the ride ~~~~~~~~~~~~~~~~~~~~~~

1. Turn right (north) out of parking lot onto Route 202. Go $\frac{4}{10}$ mile to where Route 202 turns right on Maple Street and Central Street bears slightly left.

2. Bear left on Central Street and go $\frac{4}{10}$ mile to fork where North Central Street bears left and Elmwood Road goes straight.

3. Continue straight on Elmwood Road. Go $\frac{7}{10}$ mile to fork where the main road (Forristall Road, unmarked) bears left and a smaller road goes straight up a steep hill.

4. Bear left on the main road and go $2\frac{4}{10}$ miles to wide crossroads and stop sign (Route 202). You are now in New Hampshire.

5. Cross Route 202 and go $\frac{6}{10}$ mile to where Lord Brook Road turns right and Middle Winchendon Road bears left.

6. Bear left on Middle Winchendon Road and go 1 mile to crossroads (Hunt Hill Road on left, Todd Hill Road on right).

7. Turn right on Todd Hill Road and go $\frac{7}{10}$ mile to end, at the church in the center of Rindge. At the end, notice the fine red-brick library 100 yards down the hill to your right.

8. Bear left at end on Payson Hill Road, passing an old cemetery on your right (don't turn sharply left uphill). Go $\frac{1}{2}$ mile to stop sign and blinking light at bottom of steep hill (Route 119). **CAUTION** here.

9. Cross Route 119 and go $1\frac{1}{2}$ miles to the Cathedral of the Pines on your left, midway up steep hill. Be sure to go up to the altar at the far end of the chapel to enjoy the view of the Monadnock Range.

10. Leaving the Cathedral, turn left up the hill. Go $\frac{1}{10}$ mile to Shaw Hill Road on right, at top.

11. Turn right on Shaw Hill Road and go $1\frac{9}{10}$ miles to the third left, at traffic island (Old New Ipswich Road). Cutter Hill Road bears slightly right down a steep hill at the intersection. (Note: The first left is also Old New Ipswich Road; go straight here.)

12. Turn left on Old New Ipswich Road and go $\frac{2}{10}$ mile to end (Route 119).

13. Turn left on Route 119 and go $^6/_{10}$ mile to crossroads (Converseville Road on left; Wellington Road on right).

14. Turn right on Wellington Road and go $^1/_2$ mile to fork where a dirt road bears right and the main road bears left.

15. Bear left on main road and go $^7/_{10}$ mile to another fork (Danforth Road bears right). You'll parallel the shore of Lake Monomonac 200 yards to your left.

16. Curve left at fork (still Wellington Road) and go $^1/_2$ mile to end (Main Street).

17. Turn left at end and go less than $^2/_{10}$ mile to fork where Hubbard Hill Road bears left and the main road bears right.

18. Bear right on main road and go $^7/_{10}$ mile to end (Route 202).

19. Turn left on Route 202. Go $1^7/_{10}$ miles to blinking light where Route 202 curves sharply right and Glenallen Street (unmarked) bears slightly left. You'll cross back into Massachusetts at the beginning and follow the lakeshore on your left.

20. Bear slightly left on Glenallen Street. Go $1^6/_{10}$ miles to traffic island immediately after bridge.

At this point the ride will soon follow a very poorly maintained road (hard to ride without a mountain bike) for $^9/_{10}$ mile. If you wish to avoid it (and miss Winchendon Center), bear right at traffic island and immediately bear right on Route 12. Go $^8/_{10}$ mile to Route 202 on right. Turn right, and the shopping center is on your right.

21. Bear right at traffic island and immediately cross Route 12 diagonally onto a narrow lane (Hall Road). Go $^3/_{10}$ mile to crossroads and stop sign. The Winchendon School, a coeducational preparatory school, is on your right on the far side of the golf course.

22. Go straight at crossroads $^9/_{10}$ mile to end (Teel Road). This is a steady but very gradual hill. **CAUTION:** The road is very bumpy, with wheel-eating potholes. You may wish to walk.

23. Turn right on Teel Road and go $^2/_{10}$ mile to crossroads at top of hill (Old County Road on left). This is Winchendon Center.

24. Turn right at the green on top of hill. Notice the graceful old church on your left and the fine view to your right. Go $1^1/_2$ miles to crossroads and stop sign (Route 12). This is a fine downhill run. At the bottom are a little millpond on your right and two old mills on your left.

25. Cross Route 12 onto Route 202. The shopping center is on your right.

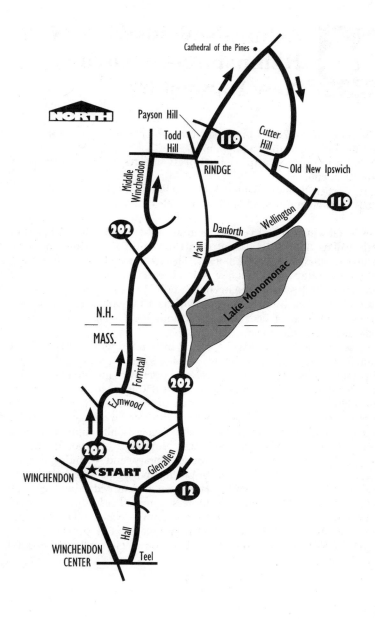

NORTH

Cathedral of the Pines •

Payson Hill

Todd
Hill

119

Cutter
Hill

Middle
Winchendon

RINDGE

Old New Ipswich

202

Danforth

Wellington

119

Main

Lake Monomonac

N.H.

MASS.

Forristall

202

Elmwood

202

202

Glenallen

★START

WINCHENDON

12

WINCHENDON
CENTER

Hall

Teel

Ashby–New Ipswich, New Hampshire–Greenville, New Hampshire

Number of miles: 26 (17 omitting New Ipswich–Greenville loop)
Terrain: Rolling, with two tough hills.
Food: Grocery in New Ipswich. Grocery and restaurant in Greenville. Grocery at end.
Start: Corner of South Road and Route 119 in the center of Ashby. Park where legal on South Road or the south side of Route 119.

This is a fascinating and very scenic tour of the rugged hills and pristine little towns north of Fitchburg in the region straddling the Massachusetts–New Hampshire border. The terrain is delightfully rolling, with some fine views from the tops of broad, open ridges. The twin towns of New Ipswich and Greenville, only 2 miles apart, contrast dramatically with each other. New Ipswich is a museum-piece rural town with an outstanding Federal-era mansion, and Greenville is a classic, well-maintained mill town.

The ride starts from Ashby, a fine little town with a classic white church and green and a rambling, wooden Victorian town hall. Outside of town you'll go along two undeveloped reservoirs and then head north into New Hampshire, skirting the base of 1,830-foot Mount Watatic, second highest mountain in the state east of the Connecticut River. Just over the border is the elegant, perfectly preserved village of New Ipswich. Gracing the center of town are two stately white churches (one of them recycled into an office building), rambling white wooden homes with dark shutters, a miniature wooden library, and a handsome brick schoolhouse at the head of a large green. And if this isn't enough, the pride of the village is the Barrett House, an elegant Federal-era mansion built in 1800 and stocked with impressive period furnishings. It is administered by the Society for the Preservation of New England Antiquities (SPNEA) and is open afternoons from June 1 to October 15.

From New Ipswich you take a short run to Greenville, a beautiful and unusually graceful old mill town. You first see it from a hillside spread out beneath you in its entirety. In the center of town is a fine Gothic-style church, gracious brick and wooden homes, an elegant inn, and an impressive high dam. A mile outside of town, in splendid isolation, is a marvelous five-story Victorian mill that's more like a castle. The return to Ashby is a delight, following the dammed-up Souhegan River and then traversing open ridges with fine views.

Directions for the rides

1. Head south on South Road and go $1/10$ mile to fork (Piper Road bears right).
2. Bear left at fork (still South Road) and go $1\,7/10$ miles to end (Richardson Road, unmarked). There's a traffic island with a monument at the intersection. You'll pass the Ashby Reservoir near the end.
3. Turn right onto Richardson and go $1\,2/10$ miles to crossroads and stop sign (Rindge Road, unmarked). You'll go along the Fitchburg Reservoir on your left. **CAUTION:** Bumps and potholes.
4. Turn right on Rindge Road and go $3\,3/10$ miles to end (Route 119), at a T-intersection. You'll pass Ward Pond on the left shortly before the end.
5. Turn right on Route 119 and go 100 yards to Pillsbury Road on left.
6. Turn left on Pillsbury Road and go 1 mile to fork (Bennett Road bears left). You can see Mount Watatic on your left.
7. Bear right at fork (still Pillsbury Road) and go $6/10$ mile to your first left (West Road, unmarked). West Road also goes straight here.
8. Turn left on West Road and go $1\,8/10$ miles to crossroads and stop sign (Ashby Road). West Road becomes Route 123A at the New Hampshire line.

When you reach Ashby Road the ride turns left, but if you wish to shorten the ride to 17 miles, turn right. Resume with direction number 16.

9. Turn left at crossroads (still Route 123A). Stay on main road for $1\,3/10$ miles to another crossroads (Smithville Road on left; Main Street on right).
10. Turn right at crossroads (still Route 123A) and go $1\,4/10$ miles to end (Routes 123 and 124). Toward the end you'll go through New Ipswich, New Hampshire, and pass the Barrett House on your left. Just before the

end there's a church on your right that has been recycled into offices. If you look to your right immediately after the church, you'll see the stately brick Appleton Academy standing proudly over the green.

11. Turn right on Routes 123 and 124. Go 100 yards to Temple Road on left, at blinking light.

12. Turn left at blinking light and go 2½ miles to end (Main Street), at stop sign, at the bottom of a steep hill. This is Greenville. At the brow of the hill, notice the Gothic-style church on your left.

13. Turn right at bottom of hill, and just ahead turn right again on Route 123 North (River Street) immediately after the bridge. There's an impressive dam on your right at the bridge. Go 1⁶⁄10 miles to end (Route 124, Turnpike Road). A splendid Victorian mill is on your right at the intersection.

14. Turn right at end and then immediately turn left uphill on River Road. Go ⁶⁄10 mile to fork where the main road bears left and a smaller road, Old Country Road, goes straight.

15. Bear left on the main road and go 1⁷⁄10 miles to crossroads and stop sign (Ashby Road). You'll pass Water Loom Pond on your left.

16. Turn left on Ashby Road (right if you're doing the short ride). Go 2⁴⁄10 miles to fork that comes up suddenly as you're going down a little hill (Simonds Road, unmarked, bears left). You are now back in Massachusetts. The first half of this stretch is a gradual climb; then you'll descend.

17. Bear left at fork and go 1 mile to end (merge left, staying on main road).

18. Bear left at end and go ⁸⁄10 mile to end (Greenville Road, Route 31).

19. Turn right on Route 31 and go 1½ miles to blinking light (Turnpike Road). It's your third crossroads. **CAUTION:** Bumpy spots.

20. Turn right on Turnpike Road and go ⁹⁄10 mile to end, at stop sign (merge right on Route 119).

21. Bear right on Route 119 and go ⁴⁄10 mile to South Road on left, in the center of Ashby. Notice the graceful brick library on your left just before the end.

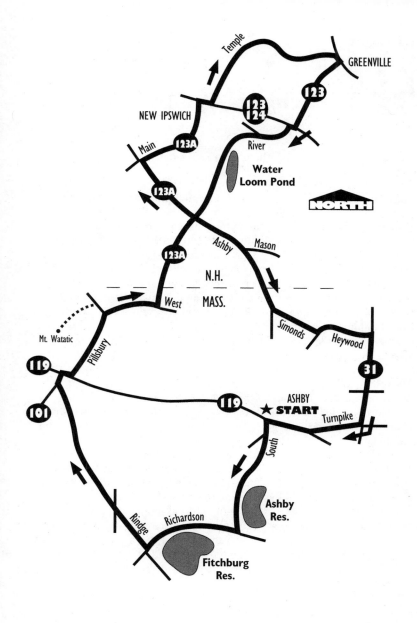

Temple

GREENVILLE

123

123
124

NEW IPSWICH

River

123A

Main

Water
Loom Pond

123A

NORTH

123A

Ashby   Mason

N.H.

West   MASS.

Mt. Watatic

Simonds   Heywood

Pillsbury

119   31

101   119   ★ ASHBY
                      START   Turnpike

South

Ashby
Res.

Rindge   Richardson

Fitchburg
Res.

Fitchburg–Ashby

Number of miles: 21 (16 without Trap Falls extension)
Terrain: Hilly.
Food: Grocery store in Ashby.
Start: Wallace Civic Center and Planetarium, John Fitch Highway, in the northeastern part of Fitchburg.
How to get there: If you're coming from the east on Route 2 or from the south on Route 190, follow Route 2 West to Route 12 North (exit 31B). Head north on Route 12 for 1⁶/₁₀ miles to crossroads and traffic light (Wanoosnoc Road on left, Bemis Road on right). Turn right and go 2⁴/₁₀ miles to civic center on right. Bemis Road becomes John Fitch Highway.

If you're coming from the west on Route 2, take the Route 31 exit (exit 28). Turn left (north) on Route 31 and go about 4 miles to downtown Fitchburg. Continue on Route 31 up a hill for 1 mile to crossroads (Rindge Road on left, John Fitch Highway on right). Turn right, and go 1 mile to civic center on left.

The rolling hills north of Fitchburg offer challenging but very scenic biking on a mazelike network of narrow, winding roads. Once you get a mile north of Fitchburg, the area is very rural, with only the tiny town of Ashby interrupting the large, sparsely populated expanses of woods and hilltop farms.

Fitchburg, a thriving industrial city of 40,000 lying in the steep valley of the North Nashua River, does not have the shabby appearance of some other mill cities in New England. The downtown area, with many fine nineteenth-century buildings flanking the main street in close formation, has been rehabilitated. A steady supply of local money has provided the city with an impressive library, civic center, planetarium, and art museum.

Fitchburg is also an active bicycling center, with some good bike shops and a thriving bicycle club. On the weekend of the Fourth of July, the city holds one of the major bicycle races in the country, attracting top-caliber contestants. If you've never seen a bike race, it's an exciting event to watch, with the racers traveling around and around a short course in a tight cluster, leaning into the corners at gravity-defying angles, and constantly jockeying for position—all at an average speed of 25 miles per hour.

Hemmed in by steep hills, Fitchburg is amazingly compact, with wooded acres within a mile of downtown. You'll start from the northern edge of the city and have a long, steady climb to a broad, rolling plateau to the north. At the top you'll go past the Fitchburg and Ashby reservoirs to the picture-book New England village of Ashby, with a pair of graceful old churches framing the small green and a handsome Victorian town hall of wood.

From Ashby you'll wind across rolling hills and small farms to Trap Falls, a picturesque little waterfall where the water cascades around both sides of a large rock. You'll return to Fitchburg along a high, open ridge with spectacular views and then enjoy a long downhill run back into the city.

Directions for the ride: 21 miles ～～～～～～～

1. Turn right out of parking lot and go 1 mile to crossroads and stop sign (Route 31).
2. Continue straight for 4$\frac{4}{10}$ miles to unmarked crossroads (Jewell Hill Road on left, Piper Road on right). The first half of this section is a long, gradual climb. Just before the crossroads, the Fitchburg Reservoir is on your right, nestled among the pines.
3. Turn right at crossroads onto Piper Road and go $\frac{4}{10}$ mile to fork (Richardson Road, unmarked, bears right).
4. Bear right on Richardson Road, following reservoir on right. Go $\frac{8}{10}$ mile to South Road, which turns left at a traffic island with a granite monument on it. **CAUTION:** Bumps and potholes.
5. Turn left on South Road and go 1$\frac{8}{10}$ miles to end (Route 119), in the center of Ashby. Just after you turn you'll pass the Ashby Reservoir on your right. When you come to the end, the handsome town hall is 200 yards to your left on Route 119. The short ride turns right on Route 119, and the long ride jogs right on Route 119 and then immediately left.
6. Turn right on Route 119 and then immediately left on New Ipswich

Road (unmarked). Go $^3/_{10}$ mile to fork at bottom of hill (Mason Road, unmarked, bears right).

7. Bear right at fork onto Mason Road and go $^3/_{10}$ mile to another fork. You come to it while you're going downhill.

8. Bear right at fork (Foster) onto Mason Road and go $1^2/_{10}$ miles to crossroads and stop sign (Greenville Road, Route 31). **CAUTION:** Bumps and potholes at the beginning.

9. Turn left on Route 31 and go $^8/_{10}$ mile to crossroads (Dump Road on left, Wheeler Road on right).

10. Turn right on Wheeler Road and go $1^2/_{10}$ miles to fork at bottom of hill (Wheeler Road bears left; Bernhardt Road bears right). Both branches are unmarked.

11. Bear right at fork onto Bernhardt Road and go $^1/_{10}$ mile to another fork (Foster Road, unmarked, bears right).

12. Bear left at fork and go $^1/_{10}$ mile to crossroads and stop sign.

13. Go straight at crossroads $^1/_{10}$ mile to end (merge right on Route 119). **CAUTION:** Steep descent with bumps and sand. At the end, you will turn sharply left.

14. Turn sharply left on Route 119. **CAUTION** here. Trap Falls is immediately ahead on your left. Continue on Route 119 for $1^7/_{10}$ miles to New Fitchburg Road on right, opposite church on left. Shortly before the intersection there's an unusual circular wooden house on the right. This is West Townsend.

15. Turn right on New Fitchburg Road and go $3^4/_{10}$ miles to Stewart Road (unmarked), which turns very sharply right. This is a pleasant run through deep pine woods, passing a state recreation area.

16. Make a very sharp right on Stewart Road and go $^3/_{10}$ mile to crossroads (Pearl Hill Road on left).

17. Turn left on Pearl Hill Road and go $2^1/_{10}$ miles to fork at bottom of long, steady hill (Fisher Road bears right downhill). You'll have a long, steady climb to the top of a ridge with magnificent views.

18. Bear *left* at fork and go $^8/_{10}$ mile to crossroads and blinking light (John Fitch Highway, unmarked).

19. Turn left on John Fitch Highway and go $^2/_{10}$ mile to civic center on left.

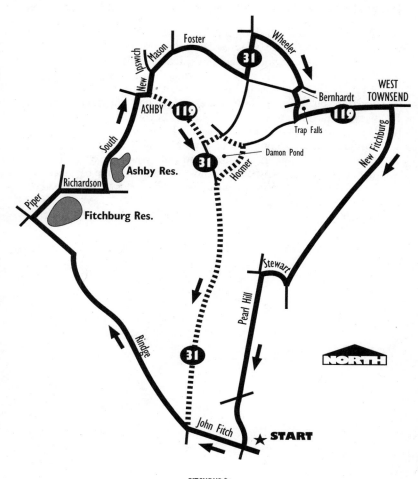

Foster

Wheeler

31

New Ipswich
Mason

WEST
TOWNSEND

Bernhardt

ASHBY

119

Trap Falls

119

South

31

Damon Pond

New Fitchburg

Ashby Res.

Hosmer

Richardson

Piper

Fitchburg Res.

Stewart

Rindge

31

Pearl Hill

NORTH

31

John Fitch

START

FITCHBURG

Directions for the ride: 16 miles

1. Follow directions for the long ride through number 5.

2. Turn right on Route 119 and go $1\frac{1}{2}$ miles to where Route 119 turns left and Route 31 South goes straight. It's all downhill!

3. Turn left on Route 119, go $\frac{1}{10}$ mile, and then turn right, staying on Route 119. Go $\frac{3}{10}$ mile to your first right (sign may say DAMON POND).

4. Turn right on this road. Immediately ahead on your right is Damon Pond, a great place for a swim on a hot day. On your left, across from the pond, a stream rushes under a small covered footbridge.

5. Continue beyond Damon Pond $\frac{6}{10}$ mile to end (merge left on Route 31). Shortly after the pond, you'll have to walk your bike around a barrier that keeps out cars. **CAUTION:** Bumps and sand near the barrier.

6. Bear left on Route 31 and go $3\frac{7}{10}$ miles to crossroads (Rindge Road on right, John Fitch Highway on left).

7. Turn left on John Fitch Highway and go 1 mile to civic center on left.

28 Athol–Royalston–Phillipston–Petersham

Number of miles: 34 (21 without Phillipston–Petersham extension)
Terrain: Hilly.
Food: Country store in South Royalston. Country store in Petersham (long ride).
Start: Victory Super Market on Route 2A in Athol, just west of the center of town. It's on the south side of the road.

This is a tour of the wooded hills northeast of the Quabbin Reservoir, passing through a trio of unspoiled, classic New England towns. A highlight of the tour is Doane Falls, a beautiful waterfall maintained by the Trustees of Reservations. The terrain is hilly, but most of the hills are gradual. Only two hills are really steep, and they are fairly short. Numerous small farms and a couple of open ridges with fine views add variety to the landscape.

The ride starts in Athol, an old mill town on the Millers River straight out of the Industrial Revolution; the grim, fortresslike mills form a nearly unbroken wall along the river for several blocks. The main industry is the manufacture of tools. In the compact downtown area, three- and four-story Victorian commercial buildings line both sides of the main street.

From Athol you'll head north, passing Tully Lake and Dam. Just ahead is Doane Falls, one of the state's unspoiled and nearly unknown beauty spots. A spectacular chain of small waterfalls, separated by deep, crystal-clear pools, flows through a wooded gorge from beneath a graceful arched stone bridge. From the falls it's not far to Royalston, one of the most elegant classic towns in the state. Commandingly located atop a hill, the town boasts a large green framed by a stately white church and gracious old wooden homes.

From Royalston you'll have a fast downhill run into South Royalston, another attractive little town with an old wooden church and schoolhouse. You'll now head along a couple of open ridges to the tiny hamlet of Phillipston, which has an old church, a cemetery, a school, and not much else. Phillipston's main claim to fame is the Baldwin Hill Bakery, a producer of good, old-fashioned stone-ground bread without the additives, preservatives, and refined-down-to-nothing flour found in most breads today.

A few miles beyond Phillipston is the dignified hilltop town of Petersham, with a large green accented by a bandstand, traditional white church, ornate stone library, and a rambling wooden building that was formerly a resort hotel. The return run to Athol leads past small farms and along a high ridge, with a fast downhill run at the end.

The short ride bypasses Phillipston and Petersham, taking a direct route back to Athol along Route 2A past the Phillipston Reservoir. There's an exhilarating downhill run at the end.

Directions for the ride: 34 miles 〰〰〰〰〰

1. Turn right (east) out of the parking lot onto Route 2A and go $^1/_{10}$ mile to traffic light.
2. Turn left at light on Exchange Street (unmarked) and go $^3/_{10}$ mile to crossroads at base of steep hill (Pequoig Avenue).
3. Turn right on Pequoig Avenue and go $^4/_{10}$ mile to end (Wellington Street). **CAUTION:** The street is bumpy.
4. Turn right on Wellington Street and go 50 yards to end (Route 32).
5. Turn left on Route 32. Just ahead, Route 32 turns left onto Silver Lake Street.
6. Turn left (still Route 32) and go $3^9/_{10}$ miles to unmarked road (Doane Hill) on right. It's the first right after you pass Tully Lake and Dam on your right.
7. Turn right on Doane Hill and go $1^2/_{10}$ miles to end, at top of steep hill. At the end you'll see an arched stone bridge on your right. Below the bridge is Doane Falls—don't miss it!
8. Turn left at end onto Athol, heading north from the falls, and go $1^9/_{10}$ miles to end (merge head-on into Route 68) in Royalston. The ride turns sharply right on Route 68, but go straight 100 yards to see the town center, one of the finest in the state.
9. Turn sharply right on Route 68. Go $4^1/_2$ miles to a road that bears right uphill shortly after a long, steep descent. The intersection is $^1/_{10}$ mile

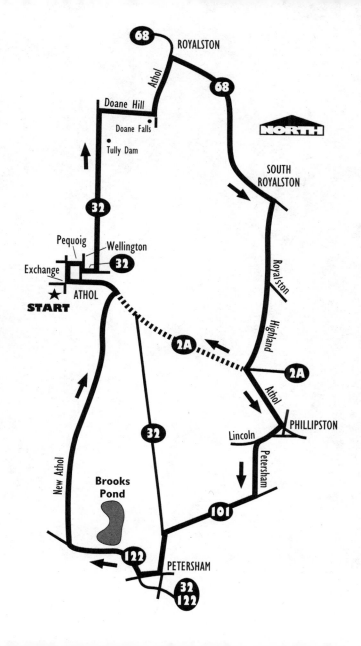

Doane Falls, Royalston

after the bridge over the Millers River in South Royalston. **CAUTION:** Diagonal railroad tracks immediately after bridge.

10. Bear right up the hill (don't turn immediately after the bridge) and go $2\frac{1}{10}$ miles to fork where the right-hand branch goes uphill. This is a pleasant run along a ridge with fine views.

11. Bear right uphill at fork and go $2\frac{1}{10}$ miles to end (Route 2A). Here the short ride turns right and the long ride turns left.

12. Turn left on Route 2A and then immediately bear right downhill on Athol Road. Go $1\frac{8}{10}$ miles to end (merge right at stop sign).

13. Bear right at end and go $\frac{1}{10}$ mile to a three-way fork. This is Phillipston. Notice the fine old church on your left.

14. Bear right at fork on Petersham Road. Go $\frac{2}{10}$ mile to another fork where the main road bears left and Lincoln Road goes straight.

15. Bear left (still Petersham Road). Go $1\frac{8}{10}$ miles to end (Route 101, Queen Lake Road), at a large, grassy traffic island.

16. Bear right on Route 101 and go $3\frac{1}{10}$ miles to end (Route 32). There's a wonderful descent at the beginning.

17. Turn left on Route 32 and go $1\frac{1}{10}$ miles to crossroads and blinking light at the center of Petersham (East Street on left; West Street on right). A country store is on the left at the intersection.

18. Turn right at crossroads and go $\frac{6}{10}$ mile to crossroads and stop sign (Route 122). **CAUTION:** It comes up while you're going down a steep hill.

19. Turn right on Route 122 and go $2\frac{2}{10}$ miles to New Athol Road, which nears right (road sign visible after you make the turn). It's your first paved road.

20. Bear right on New Athol Road and go 6 miles to end (Route 2A, Main Street). **CAUTION:** Route 2A comes up suddenly at bottom of steep hill.

21. Turn left on Route 2A and go $1\frac{4}{10}$ miles to the supermarket on your left, just beyond downtown Athol. It's a fast downhill ride back into town.

Directions for the ride: 21 miles

1. Follow the directions for the long ride through number 11.
2. Turn right on Route 2A and go $4\frac{7}{10}$ miles to the supermarket on left, just beyond downtown Athol. It's a fast downhill ride into the town.

Mount Wachusett Challenge:
West Boylston–Princeton–Sterling

Number of miles: 34 (30 if you don't go to summit)
Terrain: Guess!
Food: Grocery store and snack bar in Princeton and Sterling. Because the ride is demanding, you should carry food with you.
Start: Picnic area at the fork of Routes 12 and 140 in West Boylston, just north of the bridge over the Wachusett Reservoir. Park at side of road.

The area between Worcester and Fitchburg is dominated by 2,006-foot Mount Wachusett, the highest point in Massachusetts east of the Connecticut River. The symmetrical, gently rounded mountain, with no other mountains nearby, is a landmark for miles around. The long climb to the summit, a net gain in elevation of 1,600 feet from the starting point, offers a difficult but rewarding challenge to the adventuresome cyclist. The view from the summit, a nearly 360-degree panorama, is among the state's most spectacular. The breathtaking descent drops nearly 600 feet in the first mile, a gradient of more than 10 percent.

The ride starts from the western edge of the Wachusett Reservoir, elevation 390 feet, and follows its slender western arm to Oakdale, a small village in West Boylston. From here you'll climb gradually to Princeton, elevation 1,200 feet, along lightly traveled Route 31. The ascent does not become steep until the last quarter mile, which runs into Princeton.

Princeton is an elegantly classic New England town crowning a hillside, with a proud old church, Victorian town hall, and handsome clock-towered library poised above the large, sloping green. Before the turn of the century, Princeton was a fashionable summer resort with rambling Victorian hotels, including one on the summit of Mount Wachusett. Unfortunately, none remain.

From Princeton you'll ride along the eastern flank of the mountain, enjoying sweeping views to the east. At the beginning of the summit road is a visitor's center with exhibits on the history of the mountain and the native wildlife. The summit road climbs 800 feet in 3 miles, with most of the elevation gain in two steep sections in the first and last half mile. A succession of hotels stood on the summit until 1970, when the last one burned. The only thing up there now is a fire tower, which is not open to the public, along with a couple of radio towers.

The descent is a thriller. When you get to the end of the summit road, there's more coming—the main road drops another 400 feet in the next mile. The main entrance and base lodge of the Mount Wachusett ski area is at the bottom. You'll now pedal along lovely narrow roads, passing prosperous farms and orchards, to the attractive valley town of Sterling, which is best known as the locale of "Mary Had a Little Lamb." A small statue of a lamb on the green commemorates the nursery rhyme. From Sterling you'll return to the start, passing through woods and farmland along lightly traveled secondary roads.

Directions for the rides

1. Head north on Route 140, paralleling the western arm of the reservoir on your left. As soon as you start, notice the Old Stone Church, built in 1890, on your left. Only the stone shell remains. Go 1³/10 miles to where Route 140 curves sharply right at yield sign, in Oakdale. Continue ¹/10 mile to Laurel Street on left.
2. Turn left on Laurel Street and go 3³/10 miles to end (Route 31).
3. Turn right on Route 31 and go 5½ miles to Route 62, at blinking light in the center of Princeton. There's a country store on the far right corner. This is a good spot to get some food because the summit road begins in 3 miles.
4. Cross Route 62, following the green on your left up a steep hill. Notice the red-brick, turreted town hall, built in 1884, and the elegant stone library, built in 1883, at the end of the green. Go 3²/10 miles to the summit road on left, at top of hill (sign may say MOUNT WACHUSETT STATE RESERVATION). If you decide not to go to the summit, continue straight downhill for 1⁷/10 miles to end (Route 140), and resume with direction number 10.
5. Turn left on the summit road. The visitor's center is just ahead on your left. Be sure to get water here. Continue 2⁹/10 miles to a road on left that climbs steeply (sign says TO SUMMIT).
6. Turn left and go ²/10 mile to summit.
7. From the summit, backtrack ²/10 mile to end. Turn left and descend very steeply for ⁸/10 mile to end. **CAUTION:** Keep your speed under control.

8. Turn right and go ⁶/₁₀ mile to end, at the entrance to the state reservation.

9. Turn left and go 1⁷/₁₀ miles to end (Route 140). The first mile is a wonderful descent on smooth, aptly named Mile Hill Road. At the bottom, the Mount Wachusett Ski Area is on your left. When you come to Route 140, Wachusett Lake is on your right.

10. Turn right on Route 140 and go 2⁴/₁₀ miles to the second crossroads, Hobbs Road (it's unmarked; a sign on right may say TO SHADY LANE GREENHOUSE). **CAUTION:** Watch for potholes and cracks.

11. Turn left on Hobbs Road and go 1½ miles to an intersection where one road turns right and the other bears left uphill. **CAUTION:** Steep descent with bumps and sandy spots—take it easy.

12. Bear left uphill and follow the main road 5¹/₁₀ miles to end, in Sterling (merge right on Routes 12 and 62). Two smaller roads bear left on this stretch, but go straight on the main road at both intersections. The first ½ mile climbs steeply—a piece of cake compared to Mount Wachusett. Just before the end, you'll go along the Sterling town green on your left.

13. Bear right at end and go ¹/₁₀ mile to fork where Route 12 bears left and Route 62 bears right.

14. Bear right on Route 62 and go ⁴/₁₀ mile to Jewett Road (unmarked) on left.

15. Turn left on Jewett Road and go 1 mile to a five-way intersection, at stop sign.

16. Turn 90 degrees left immediately after the stop sign, staying on Jewett Road. Don't turn sharply left directly at the stop sign. Go ¼ mile to end, at stop sign (merge right onto Route 12).

17. Bear right on Route 12 and go ¹/₁₀ mile to Bean Road, which bears right.

18. Bear right on Bean Road and go ¼ mile to a diagonal crossroads and stop sign.

19. Continue straight for 2⁴/₁₀ miles to end, at stop sign (merge right on Route 12). **CAUTION:** Bumpy railroad tracks at bottom of hill after 1 mile.

20. Bear right on Route 12 and go ²/₁₀ mile to starting point.

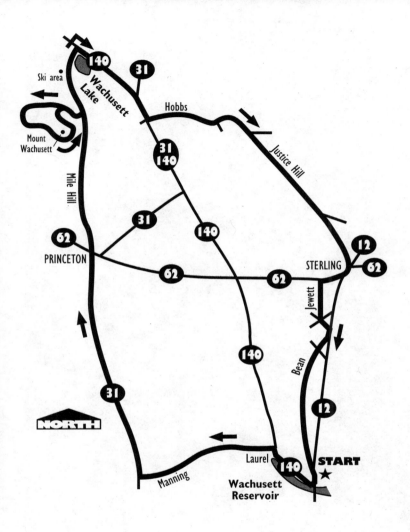

140
31
Ski area
Wachusett Lake
Hobbs
Justice Hill
Mount Wachusett
31 140
Mile Hill
31
140
62
12
PRINCETON
62
STERLING
62
Jewett
140
Bean
140
12
NORTH
31
Laurel
140
START
Manning
Wachusett Reservoir

Ware River Bridge, Gilbertville

Covered-Bridge Ride:
Ware–Hardwick–Gilbertville

Number of miles: 28 (16 without northern loop)
Terrain: Hilly.
Food: Country store in Hardwick. Grocery and snack bar in Gilbertville. Friendly's at end.
Start: Municipal parking lot in downtown Ware, on the north side of Route 9. It's between Friendly's and the Casino movie theater, opposite Route 32 South.

The section of Massachusetts between Worcester and the Quabbin Reservoir provides challenging but extremely scenic cycling. This is a very rural area of high, open ridges with spectacular views, dotted with unspoiled, picture-book New England towns. The cycle of tough climb, plateau atop a ridge, and exhilarating descent repeats itself as you wind through the inspiring landscape on untraveled back roads. On this ride you explore the area fairly close to the reservoir, passing through the classic village of Hardwick and then across one of only two covered bridges in the state east of the Connecticut River (the other is in Pepperell).

You start from Ware, a nineteenth-century mill town right out of the Industrial Revolution. Most of the mills have factory outlets selling to the public, making Ware one of the prime bargain centers in New England for clothing, woolen goods, and sportswear. The majority of the mills are clustered in one massive complex called the Industry Yard on Route 9 just east of downtown.

From Ware you quickly head into ridge country to Hardwick, a beautiful classic town among the many spread across Worcester County. The large, well-kept green is framed by two graceful old churches facing each other and by the handsome, white, pillared town hall. From Hardwick you'll traverse a ridge with inspiring views and enjoy a long descent into Gilbertville, a small, attractive mill town with a magnificent stone church. In Gilbertville you'll cross the Ware River over the covered bridge and return to Ware across yet another ridge along a narrow country lane.

163

The longer ride makes a loop north of Hardwick through more ridge-and-valley country. As you head north out of Hardwick, you come closer to the Quabbin Reservoir and catch glimpses of it far below. At the northern tip of the ride, you can go a quarter of a mile off the route to the water's edge. From here you'll return to Hardwick along ridges with fine views.

Directions for the ride: 28 miles

1. Turn right out of parking lot onto Route 9 and right immediately after movie theater on Parker Street. Go $\frac{1}{10}$ mile to end (Pleasant Street, unmarked).

2. Turn left at end and go $\frac{1}{2}$ mile to fork where Crescent Street bears left and Greenwich Road bears right. You'll pass an attractive little dam on your right.

3. Bear right at fork, passing a cemetery on your left, and go $2\frac{3}{10}$ miles to Hardwick Pond Road, which bears right.

4. Bear right on Hardwick Pond Road and go $3\frac{1}{2}$ miles to end (merge head-on into Route 32A). This is a winding narrow lane ascending gradually onto a ridge with fine views. **CAUTION:** Bumpy and sandy spots.

5. Go straight onto Route 32A for $1\frac{2}{10}$ miles to Barre Road on right, in the center of Hardwick. Here the short ride turns right and the long ride continues straight.

6. Continue straight on Route 32A for $\frac{4}{10}$ mile to fork (North Road bears right). At the beginning on your left is an ornate brick library with a cupola.

7. Bear left at fork (still Route 32A) and go $4\frac{8}{10}$ miles to a road on the right at the bottom of the second long descent (a worn sign may say TO BARRE). Here the ride turns right, but if you turn left at the intersection on a dirt path and proceed $\frac{3}{10}$ mile you'll come to the eastern arm of the Quabbin Reservoir.

8. Turn right at bottom of hill and go $\frac{9}{10}$ mile to fork (Old Dana Road, unmarked, bears right uphill). It's a steady climb to the fork.

9. Bear right uphill and go $\frac{1}{2}$ mile to Spring Hill Road on right, at top of hill.

10. Turn right on Spring Hill Road and go 5 miles to end, at yield sign (merge left onto Route 32A).

11. Bear left on 32A and go $\frac{3}{10}$ mile to fork at the Hardwick town green

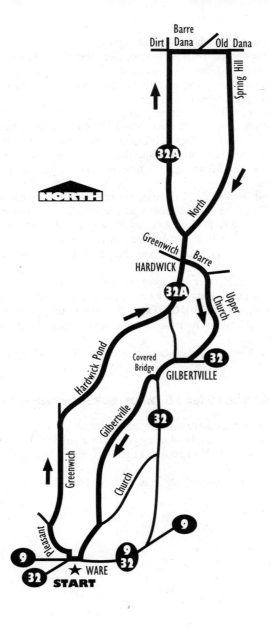

(Route 32A, unmarked here, bears slightly right).

12. Bear left at fork and go $^1/_{10}$ mile to end. Here the ride turns left, but there's a country store 100 yards to your right.

13. Turn left at end onto Barre and go $^4/_{10}$ mile to fork where Upper Church Street bears right uphill.

14. Bear right on Upper Church Street and go $2^8/_{10}$ miles to end (merge right at stop sign on Route 32, Lower Road). This is another pleasant, narrow lane, climbing onto a ridge with great views. After you crest the ridge, a relaxing downhill run takes you to the Ware River Valley.

15. Bear right on Route 32 and go $^2/_{10}$ mile to end (merge left at stop sign). This is Gilbertville.

16. Bear left at end (still Route 32). After $^2/_{10}$ mile you'll cross the Ware River. **CAUTION:** Diagonal railroad tracks immediately after bridge. Continue less than $^2/_{10}$ mile to Bridge Street on right (sign may say COVERED BRIDGE). You can see the bridge from the corner. Here the ride turns right, but you'll find a magnificent stone church if you go straight 200 yards.

17. Turn right on Bridge Street and cross the covered bridge, one of only ten remaining in Massachusetts. Continue $3^1/_{10}$ miles to end (merge to your right while going downhill). **CAUTION:** Watch for bumpy spots.

18. Bear right at end and go $^8/_{10}$ mile to traffic light (Route 9). This is a nice downhill run.

19. Turn right on Route 9 and go less than $^2/_{10}$ mile to parking lot on right.

Directions for the ride: 16 miles

1. Follow directions for the long ride through number 5.

2. Turn right on Barre Road. As soon as you turn a country store is on your right. Go $^1/_2$ mile to fork where Upper Church Street bears right uphill.

3. Follow directions for the long ride from number 14 to the end.

Central Massachusetts Spectacular:
North Brookfield–New Braintree–Barre–Oakham

Number of miles: 30
Terrain: Hilly.
Food: Grocery and snack bar in Barre.
Start: Center of North Brookfield, on Route 67. You can park without time restrictions on School Street, the cross street on the east side of Route 67.

The rolling, open hills, ridges, and valleys midway between Worcester and Springfield provide some of the most inspiring scenery in Massachusetts. Of all the rides in this book, this one is my favorite. The terrain is challenging—a recurrent cycle of steep climbs and exhilarating descents—but the panoramic vistas from atop every hill will more than reward your efforts. Here is rural countryside at its best: rambling old farmhouses, weathered red barns with woodpiles neatly stacked beside them, stone walls zigzagging across broad, sloping fields where cows and horses graze. Dotting this Currier-and-Ives landscape are unspoiled museum-piece towns and hamlets, hardly changed since the 1800s.

The ride starts from one of these towns, North Brookfield, a New England jewel with a stately old church and green, a handsome stone library, and an ornate Victorian town hall built in 1864. When the Rolling Stones needed a place to practice for their 1981 American tour, they chose North Brookfield. From here you'll bike across ridgetops and along two delightful ponds to Oakham, a pristine hilltop hamlet buried off the beaten path among a maze of back roads. No one would ever find it except by accident. A graceful white church, fine stone library, schoolhouse, and old cemetery make up the village center. From Oakham you'll wind your way on deserted country lanes to the larger town of Barre, also a New England classic. The extensive green, ornamented with a bandstand in the center, forms a nucleus from which eight roads radiate like spokes. Adjoining the green are a stately wooden church, an old town hall, and a compact little business block.

From Barre you'll traverse more ridges with sweeping views to the nearly depopulated hamlet of New Braintree. The center of town has a fine white church, an old cemetery, a tiny post office, a handful of weathered farmhouses, and not much else. The training academy for the state police stands on a hilltop a short distance south of the village center (a Seventh-Day Adventist academy formerly stood on the site). From New Braintree, we're soon back to North Brookfield, biking through magnificently rolling, open farmland.

Directions for the ride

1. Head north (uphill) on Route 67 and go $7/10$ mile to Route 148 North (Oakham Road), which bears right.
2. Bear right on Route 148 and go $5\,3/10$ miles to second crossroads (Spencer Road on right, Ware Corner Road on left). You'll pass Doane Pond on the left after about a mile.
3. Turn left at crossroads onto Ware Corner and go $1\,1/10$ miles to Maple Street on left, at top of hill. This is the center of Oakham. Notice the fine stone library on your left at the intersection. This stretch is a steady climb.
4. Turn left on Maple Street and go $1/10$ mile to your first right.
5. Turn right (still Maple Street). Go $8/10$ mile to unmarked fork where Adams Road goes straight and the main road (Barre Road) bears right. There's a steep descent at the beginning.
6. Bear right on the main road and go $8/10$ mile to end (Old Turnpike Road, unmarked).
7. Turn left at end onto Old Turnpike Road and go $2/10$ mile to Hunt Road (unmarked) on right. A country store is immediately after the intersection on the right.
8. Turn right on Hunt Road and go $1/2$ mile to fork where the main road curves left downhill.
9. Curve left on main road. Go $3/10$ mile to another fork where Happy Hollow Road turns left and the main road bears right. Notice the unusual stone tower on your right as you're going down the hill.
10. Bear right on main road (still Hunt Road) and go 1 mile to stop sign at bottom of hill (merge right). **CAUTION:** Steep descent with sharp curves, bumps, and sandy spots—take it easy. From the top of the hill you can see Mount Wachusett, the highest mountain in central Massachusetts, elevation 2,006 feet.

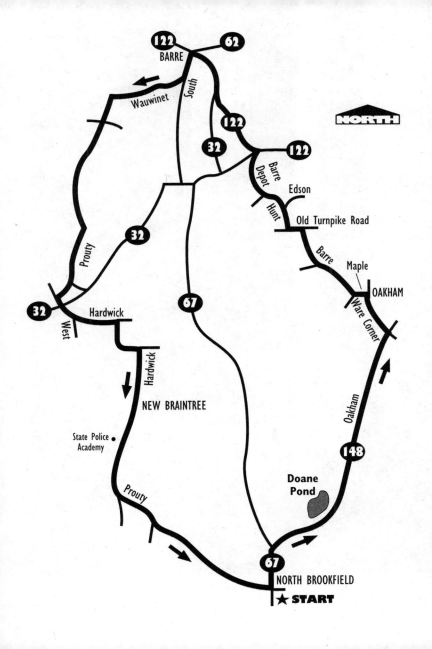

Dairy farm in Rutland

11. Bear right at bottom of hill and go $^1/_{10}$ mile to end (Route 122). You'll cross the Ware River; notice the dam on your right as you cross the bridge.

12. Turn left on Route 122 and go $2^9/_{10}$ miles into the center of Barre. Follow Route 122 alongside the green, passing the bandstand on your left.

13. At the far end of the green, turn sharply left, passing the Barre Historical Society, a white mansion with columns, on your right. Continue $^6/_{10}$ mile to Wauwinet Road, which bears right while you're going uphill. You'll pass the Cook's Canyon Audubon preserve on the left. The name is an exaggeration—the canyon is a small ravine with a brook trickling through it.

14. Bear right on Wauwinet Road and go $2^1/_2$ miles to crossroads and stop sign (Cutler Road on left, Hardwick Road on right).

15. Go straight at crossroads and stay on the main road for $4^1/_{10}$ miles to end, at bottom of hill. **CAUTION** here—the end comes up suddenly. At the end of this stretch you'll enjoy a long descent with magnificent views.

16. Turn left at end and go $^1/_{10}$ mile to crossroads and stop sign (Route 32, Lower Road).

17. Cross Route 32. After $^3/_{10}$ mile, West Road bears right, but continue straight for $^9/_{10}$ mile to your next right (Hardwick Road, unmarked), which crosses a small bridge.

18. Turn right on Hardwick Road. After $^6/_{10}$ mile the main road curves 90 degrees left uphill. Continue $^1/_2$ mile to your first right, at a spot where the hill levels off a bit. Notice the white, pillared mansion on your left at the intersection.

19. Turn right on this road and go $3^2/_{10}$ miles to fork at bottom of long hill (West Brookfield Road bears right, Prouty Road bears left). You'll go through New Braintree and pass the state police training academy.

20. Bear left at fork onto Prouty Road and follow the main road $3^4/_{10}$ miles back to Route 67, in the center of North Brookfield. Some smaller roads branch off, but stay on the main road. There's a steep climb into town.

Worcester–Paxton–Holden–Rutland

Number of miles: 30 (24 with shortcut, 13 without Paxton–Rutland extension)
Terrain: Hilly.
Food: Grocery stores and snack bars in the towns.
Start: Corner of Pleasant Street and Tiverton Parkway in the western part of Worcester, just east of Route 122 (Chandler Street). Park on Tiverton Parkway. From Route 290, head west on Route 122. After 2 miles you'll pass Worcester State College. Continue nearly 1 mile to traffic light where Route 122 turns left and Pleasant Street turns right. Turn right, and Tiverton Parkway is the first left.

Just northwest of Worcester is a prime area for cycling. It has wooded hills interspersed with ponds and reservoirs, occasional open ridges with fine views, and unspoiled towns that haven't yet become suburban. Worcester is fortunate to be a relatively compact city with almost no suburban sprawl beyond its borders. Within a mile of the start you're in wooded countryside before you even cross the city line.

The ride starts from the Tatnuck section of Worcester, near its western edge, and almost immediately enters forested landscape. Just off the route near the beginning is the Cascade, a steep, rocky ravine that becomes a dramatic waterfall after heavy rain and a delicate, icy fairyland in the winter. Just beyond the city line you'll enjoy a long, exhilarating run beside the Holden Reservoirs. Go across the Kendall Reservoir and arrive in Holden, an attractive community with two graceful old churches and a Federal-era mansion framing the center of town. From Holden you'll enjoy a gradual descent back into Worcester and return to the start through gracious residential neighborhoods.

The long ride heads farther west and north to the graceful old town of Paxton. Although less than 10 miles from downtown Worcester, Paxton remains an unspoiled New England gem of a town with a stately white church, an old town hall, fine white wooden homes, and the gracious Paxton Inn, all clustered around the village center. From Paxton you'll head north over hill, dale, and ridge to Rutland, another refreshingly unspoiled town crowning a hilltop. From Rutland you'll thread your way to Holden along a labyrinth of winding, roller-coasting lanes. In Holden you'll pick up the short ride and follow it back to Worcester.

Directions for the rides: 30 and 24 miles 〰〰〰

1. Turn right (downhill) on Pleasant Street, and immediately bear right at traffic light on Mower Street. Go $^2/_{10}$ mile to fork (Olean Street bears right).

2. Bear right on Olean Street. Stay on the main road for $2^9/_{10}$ miles to fork where South Road (unmarked) bears left uphill. **CAUTION:** The edge of the road at the beginning is bumpy from sewer construction. This is a beautiful run along the Holden Reservoirs.

   If you're taking the ride after a heavy rain, be sure to visit the Cascade. After bearing right on Olean Street, take your first left on Fernside Road. Go to end, turn right and immediately left on Windemere Road, and go to end. Turn right and go $^3/_{10}$ mile to Cascade on left. Backtrack to Olean Street.

3. Bear left on South Road and go 1 mile to end (Route 31). At the end, the 13-mile ride turns right on Route 31 and the longer rides turn left.

4. Turn left on Route 31 and go $1^6/_{10}$ miles to end, at stop sign and blinking light.

5. Turn left at end (still Route 31) and go $^2/_{10}$ mile to where Route 31 turns right onto Maple Street.

6. Turn right, staying on Route 31, and go $^1/_2$ mile to end (Route 56, Richards Avenue). This is Paxton. The center of town is on your left. Notice the fine church to your left at the intersection.

7. Turn right on Route 56 and go $4^7/_{10}$ miles to end (Route 122A, Main Street), in the center of Rutland. Here the 30-mile ride turns left, but you can shorten the route by 6 miles if you turn right on Route 122A, go $1^7/_{10}$ miles to Bond Road on right at the Holden town line, and resume with direction number 13.

8. Turn left on Routes 56 and 122A. Just ahead, Route 56 turns right, and Route 122A goes straight.

9. Turn right on Route 56 and go $3^3/_{10}$ miles to Campbell Street on right, $^1/_2$ mile after Edison Pond on right. There's a great downhill run out of

Rutland, and you'll pass Moulton Pond at the bottom.

10. Turn right on Campbell Street and go 1⁸⁄₁₀ miles to end (merge right on Glenwood Road). There is no stop sign here.

11. Bear right on Glenwood Road and go 1½ miles to end (Route 122A).

12. Turn left on Route 122A and go 1 mile to Bond Road on right, at the Holden town line.

13. Turn right on Bond Road. After ³⁄₁₀ mile the road turns 90 degrees right. Continue ⁴⁄₁₀ mile to end (Hillside Road).

14. Turn left on Hillside Road and go 3¹⁄₁₀ miles to fork immediately after you pass between two ponds (Hilltop Avenue, unmarked, bears right). **CAUTION:** Bumpy and sandy spots.

15. Bear left at fork and go ²⁄₁₀ mile to end (Route 122A).

16. Turn right on Route 122A and go 1½ miles to traffic light (Route 31) in the center of Holden. Just before the light you'll pass two graceful churches and a Federal-era mansion on your left.

17. Cross Route 31 and go ⁷⁄₁₀ mile to Salisbury Street, which bears right at traffic light.

18. Bear right on Salisbury Street and go 4⁴⁄₁₀ miles to Flagg Street on right, shortly after Assumption College on left. You'll pass Dawson Pond on the right after ⁶⁄₁₀ mile. Notice the handsome. domed Albanian Orthodox church on the right ⁴⁄₁₀ mile before the intersection.

19. Turn right on Flagg Street and go ⁴⁄₁₀ mile to fork (Richmond Avenue, unmarked, bears left).

20. Bear right at fork (still Flagg Street) and go ½ mile to crossroads and stop sign (Pleasant Street).

21. Turn right on Pleasant Street and go ⁷⁄₁₀ mile to Tiverton Parkway on right.

Directions for the ride: 13 miles 〰〰〰〰〰〰

1. Follow directions for the long rides through number 3.

2. Turn right on Route 31 and go 2½ miles to traffic light (Route 122A). This is the center of Holden. At the intersection, notice the two fine churches and the Federal-era mansion to your left on Route 122A.

3. Turn right on Route 122A and go ⁷⁄₁₀ mile to Salisbury Street, which bears right at traffic light.

4. Follow directions for the long rides from number 18 to the end.

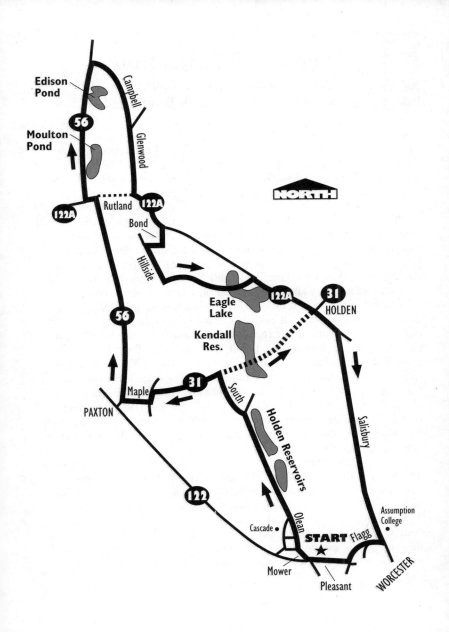

Edison
Pond

56

Moulton
Pond

Campbell

Glenwood

122A   Rutland   **122A**

Bond

Hillside

Eagle
Lake   **122A**   **31**
HOLDEN

Kendall
Res.

56

Maple   **31**

South

PAXTON

Salisbury

Holden Reservoirs

122

Olean

Cascade •

Assumption
College •

START Flagg

Mower

Pleasant

WORCESTER

NORTH

The Brookfields Ride:
East Brookfield–Brookfield–
West Brookfield–North Brookfield

Number of miles: 26 (22 omitting western loop)
Terrain: Delightfully rolling, with several short hills and one tough one.
Food: Groceries and restaurants in the towns, except Brookfield.
Start: Park on Route 9 beside Lake Lashaway in the center of East Brookfield. East Brookfield is about 15 miles west of Worcester.

On this ride you explore the four similarly named towns midway between Worcester and Springfield. The surrounding landscape, a harmonious mixture of magnificent rolling farmland, wooded hills, ridges with inspiring views, and several lakes, promises biking at its best along a wide-ranging network of rural lanes and lightly traveled secondary roads. The terrain is not as hilly as the more rugged ridge country surrounding it.

The rides start in East Brookfield, smallest and least distinctive of the quartet, attractively located along the shore of Lake Lashaway. A couple of miles out of town is a fine run along Quaboag Pond, largest lake in the area, followed by another run beside Quacumquasit Pond (say it three times fast). From here you'll ascend gradually onto a hillside with magnificent views across the well-groomed fields of estates and horse farms. Just ahead you'll cross the Quaboag River and climb a short hill into the classic New England village of Brookfield. The long, slender green is framed by two dignified churches, an ornate brick Victorian library, and fine old homes. Just off the green, the compact business block is a relic from the turn of the century.

Leaving Brookfield, you'll climb onto another ridge with fine views and descend into West Brookfield, most elegant of the four towns. The long, triangular green, highlighted by a fountain in the middle, is surrounded by a fine church and gracious wooden and brick homes. Just west of town you'll make a circuit around Wickaboag Pond and thread your way between rolling hills to North Brookfield, yet another New England gem of a town, with a traditional white church and green, graceful stone library, and an ornate Victorian town hall with a bell tower, built in 1864. A statue on the green honors the soldiers killed in the War of the Rebellion, the official Union name for the Civil War.

From North Brookfield you'll enjoy a relaxing downhill run through orchards back to the shore of Lake Lashaway and East Brookfield.

Directions for the rides ୬୬୬୬୬୬୬୬୬୬୬୬୬

1. Head west on Route 9 and go $2^1/_{10}$ miles to Quaboag Street on left. It's your first left after the Brookfield town line, and it immediately crosses a railroad bridge.

2. Turn left on Quaboag Street and stay on the main road for $2^1/_{10}$ miles to West Sturbridge Road on right, at top of hill. You'll go along Quaboag Pond on your right.

3. Turn right on West Sturbridge Road and go $1^7/_{10}$ miles to fork where West Sturbridge Road bears left and South Pond Road bears right.

4. Bear right at fork onto South Pond Road and go $^7/_{10}$ mile to Lake Road (unmarked), which bears right after you pass Quacumquasit Pond on your left.

5. Bear right on Lake Road and go $2^1/_{10}$ miles to end, where you'll merge to the right at bottom of hill on Rice Corner Road (no stop sign here).

6. Bear right at end and go $^1/_4$ mile to end (merge right on Route 148 at stop sign).

7. Bear right on Route 148 and go $1^1/_{10}$ miles to end (Route 9). At the end you'll go along the Brookfield town green. Notice the Victorian library on the right at beginning of green.

8. Turn left on Route 9 and go $^6/_{10}$ mile to West Brookfield Road, which bears right.

9. Bear right on West Brookfield Road and go $1^7/_{10}$ miles to end, at stop sign (merge right on Route 9). This is another pleasant road climbing onto a ridge with fine views, passing fields bordered by graceful rows of shade trees.

10. Bear right on Route 9 and go $^3/_{10}$ mile to end of green in West Brookfield (Route 67 turns sharply right). Here the longer ride goes straight, but, if you wish, you can chop off 4 miles by turning sharply right on Route 67, going $1^2/_{10}$ miles to Hunt Road on left, and resuming with direction number 15.

11. Continue straight on Route 9 for $1^8/_{10}$ miles to Snow Road on right.

You'll pass Wickaboag Pond on your right. If you come to the Salem Cross Inn (a well-known, elegant restaurant), you've gone $^2/_{10}$ mile too far.

12. Turn right on Snow Road and go $1^2/_{10}$ miles to end (Wickaboag Valley).

13. Turn right at end onto Wickaboag Valley and go $1^9/_{10}$ miles to crossroads and stop sign (Route 67), staying on main road. You'll pass Wickaboag Pond again. At the crossroads, the West Brookfield town green is on the far right corner.

14. Turn left on Route 67 and go 1 mile to Hunt Road on left.

15. Turn left on Hunt Road and go $^1/_2$ mile to fork (Old West Brookfield Road bears right).

16. Bear right at fork onto Old West Brookfield Road and go $^6/_{10}$ mile to another fork at triangular traffic island (Cider Mill Road bears right).

17. Bear left at fork (don't turn left immediately before it). Go $^2/_{10}$ mile to the next intersection, where Tucker Hill Road turns left and the main road bears right.

18. Bear right on main road and go $^8/_{10}$ mile to crossroads and stop sign (Route 67).

19. Turn left on Route 67 and go $^1/_2$ mile to stop sign at top of hill (Route 67 turns left).

20. Turn left at stop sign (still Route 67) and go $^1/_{10}$ mile to crossroads (Summer Street on left; School Street on right). This is North Brookfield. Notice the marvelous town hall on the far left corner.

21. Turn right at crossroads onto School Street and go $^2/_{10}$ mile to fork (Elm Street bears right).

22. Bear right at fork onto Elm Street. Go $2^7/_{10}$ miles to traffic island where North Street (unmarked) turns right and the main road bears left. It's just after bottom of long hill.

23. Bear left on main road and go $^8/_{10}$ mile to a road on your right that crosses a small bridge. You'll pass Lake Lashaway on your right.

24. Turn right on this road, following the lake on your right. After 1 mile Harrington Lane, a dead-end road, bears right. Bear left on main road and go $^1/_{10}$ mile to end (Route 9).

25. Turn right on Route 9 and go $^8/_{10}$ mile back to start.

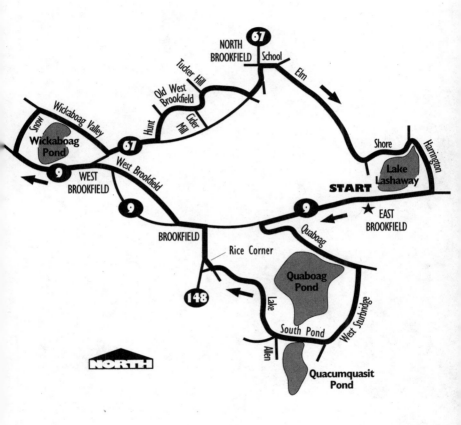

67

NORTH
BROOKFIELD   School

Tucker Hill   Elm

Old West
Brookfield

Wickaboag Valley   Hunt   Cider Mill

Snow

Wickaboag
Pond   67   Shore   Harrington

West Brookfield   Lake
Lashaway

9   WEST
BROOKFIELD   START

9   EAST
BROOKFIELD

BROOKFIELD   Quaboag

Rice Corner

148   Lake   Quaboag
Pond

West Sturbridge

South Pond

Allen

Quacumquasit
Pond

NORTH

Llama farm in Leicester

West of Worcester:
Spencer–Paxton–Leicester

Number of miles: 25 (15 without Paxton extension)
Terrain: Hilly.
Food: Groceries and restaurants in the towns.
Start: Municipal parking lot at the intersection of Routes 9 and 31 North in Spencer. Entrance is on Route 31 North.

The region just west of Worcester, a harmonious mixture of rolling farmland and woods dotted with ponds, provides very scenic biking on a network of traffic-free rural roads. Although close to the city, the area is pleasantly rural because Worcester is fortunate in not being surrounded by dreary, sprawling suburbs. In addition to the countryside, two landmarks highlight this ride: a Trappist monastery and the fine Moore State Park.

The ride starts from Spencer, an attractive, compact mill town clinging to steep hillsides, located about 12 miles west of Worcester. A magnificent old church, a nineteenth-century brick business block, fine old Victorian homes, and an ornate wooden hotel give charm to the town. A few miles north of town is one of the state's more unusual places of interest, Saint Joseph's Abbey, a Trappist monastery. The church, which is open to the public, is a large, impressive stone building with an interior shrouded in nearly total darkness. Inside, the silence is overpowering. The monks sing Gregorian chants at their services every couple of hours throughout the day, beginning with vigils at 3:30 in the morning. To listen to these slow, unaccompanied intonations in the darkness is a haunting experience. At the entrance to the grounds is a gift shop selling recordings of Gregorian chants, religious articles, and jams and preserves made by the monks. A monk in full, flowing robes, grim and gaunt as a cadaver, minds the shop.

A few miles beyond the monastery is a brighter spot, Moore State Park. Here a stream cascades in a file of waterfalls past a beautifully restored old mill. Above the mill is a small millpond. From here it's not far to the graceful town of Paxton, another mostly rural community less than 10 miles from downtown Worcester. A traditional wooden church, an old town hall, some fine, white wooden homes, and the elegant Paxton Inn grace the center of town.

From Paxton you have an enjoyable ride to the handsome hilltop town of Leicester along the shores of several ponds. Although its town center is only 7 miles from downtown Worcester, Leicester is a surprisingly unspoiled rural community. The large rectangular green is framed by an impressive stone church and the campus of Becker College. From Leicester you'll head past Cedar Meadow Pond and Stiles Reservoir back to Spencer.

The short ride bypasses Paxton by heading from Spencer directly toward Leicester. After about 2 miles on Route 9 (which has a wide shoulder), you'll get onto back roads that go past a llama farm and weave through fine rolling farmland.

Directions for the ride: 25 miles 〰〰〰〰〰

1. Turn left out of parking lot onto Route 31 North. (The short ride starts off by heading east on Route 9.) Go 5²/₁₀ miles to crossroads (Browning Pond Road on left; Thompson's Pond Road on right). The entrance road to Saint Joseph's Abbey is on the left after 3⁹/₁₀ miles. It's ⁹/₁₀ mile up a steady hill to the abbey church, with a steep pitch at the end.
2. Turn right at crossroads onto Thompson's Pond Road up a steep hill and go 1⁸/₁₀ miles to South Street on left. You'll cross Thompson's Pond.
3. Turn left on South Street and go ⁷/₁₀ mile to end (Route 31).
4. Turn left on Route 31 and go ½ mile to Black Hill Road, which bears right while you're going downhill. It's the second road that bears right.
5. Bear right on Black Hill Road and go ²/₁₀ mile to bridge. **CAUTION:** Bumps and potholes. Be sure to look to your right at the bridge; there's a fine view of the waterfall and the old mill in Moore State Park.
6. Just after the bridge, make a hairpin right turn onto a narrow lane that passes through a pair of stone pillars (don't turn 90 degrees right onto Brigham Road). The lane is blocked off to cars. You'll have to walk your bike; there's a NO VEHICLES sign at the other end of the lane. You wouldn't want to ride up that hill anyway. Follow the lane through Moore State Park for ½ mile to end (merge left onto Route 31).

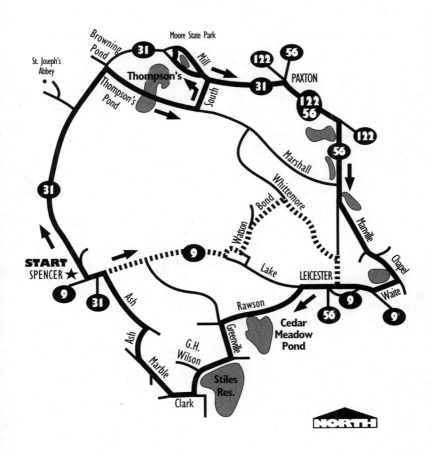

7. Bear left on Route 31 and go 1^3/$_{10}$ miles to traffic light in the center of Paxton (Route 122).

8. Turn right on Route 122 and go 1^3/$_{10}$ miles to crossroads where Route 56 (Reservoir Drive) turns right.

9. Turn right on Route 56 and go 1^8/$_{10}$ miles to Manville Street (unmarked), which bears left along a reservoir. It's shortly after a crossroads. You'll pass two reservoirs bordered by stately groves of pines.

10. Bear left on Manville Street, following the water on your left, and go 1^1/$_2$ miles to end, at stop sign.

11. Turn left at end and go 100 yards to fork (Mulberry Street bears left; Chapel Street bears right).

12. Bear right at fork and go ^{1}/$_2$ mile to Waite Street (unmarked) on right, just beyond Waite Pond.

13. Turn right on Waite Street and go ^{4}/$_{10}$ mile to end (Route 9). Notice the handsome brick church in front of you at the end.

14. Bear right on Route 9 and go ^{2}/$_{10}$ mile to where Route 9 curves left and Main Street bears right up a hill.

15. Bear right on Main Street and go ^{1}/$_2$ mile to stop sign (merge head-on into Route 9). You'll climb steeply at the beginning and pass Becker College and the Leicester town green on your right at the top of the hill.

16. Go straight on Route 9 for ^{1}/$_2$ mile to crossroads (Lake Avenue on right, Rawson Street on left). It's just after the Castle Restaurant on the right. Notice the handsome stone library on your right at the beginning.

17. Turn left on Rawson Street. Stay on the main road for 2^2/$_{10}$ miles to end (Greenville Road, unmarked. The end is almost a crossroads—Kingsbury Road continues on the far side of the intersection about 20 feet to your right). You'll climb steeply for ^{3}/$_{10}$ mile near the beginning and pass Cedar Meadow Pond on your left toward the end.

18. Turn left on Greenville Road and go ^{8}/$_{10}$ mile to end (Chickering Road). The Stiles Reservoir is in front of you at the end.

19. Turn right at end and go ^{1}/$_2$ mile to fork (G. H. Wilson Road bears right).

20. Bear left at fork, following the water on your left, and go ^{6}/$_{10}$ mile to end (Clark Road).

21. Turn right at end onto Clark Road and go ^{3}/$_{10}$ mile to your first right, Marble Road.

22. Turn right on Marble Road and go ^{8}/$_{10}$ mile to end (merge right; no stop sign). **CAUTION:** Watch for bumps and potholes.

23. Bear right at end and go ½ mile to Ash Street, which bears right.

24. Bear right on Ash Street and go ⁷/₁₀ mile to a wide fork (R. Jones Road on right).

25. Turn left at end (still Ash Street) and go 1⁴/₁₀ miles to end (Route 9, Main Street). At the end a beautiful old church is to your right on Route 9.

26. Turn left on Route 9 and go ³/₁₀ mile to second traffic light, at the bottom of a steep hill, where Route 31 North (Pleasant Street) turns right. You're back in the center of Spencer. Notice the fine Victorian homes along Route 9 and the ornate hotel at the corner of Route 31.

27. Turn right on Route 31 and immediately left into parking lot. Notice the turreted library opposite the entrance to the lot.

Directions for the ride: 15 miles 🌊🦆🦆🦆🦆🦆🦆🦆

1. Turn right out of parking lot and immediately left (east) on Route 9. Go 2³/₁₀ miles to unmarked road on left immediately after the Leicester town line.

2. Turn left and go ²/₁₀ mile to Watson Street on left.

3. Turn left on Watson Street. Stay on the main road for ½ mile to fork where Moose Hill Road bears left and Bond Street bears right. You'll pass a llama farm on your left just after you turn onto Watson Street.

4. Bear right on Bond Street and go ⁷/₁₀ mile to end, at traffic island (Whittemore Street, unmarked).

5. Turn right at end onto Whittemore Street. Go 1⁹/₁₀ miles to end (Route 56), passing through splendid rolling farmland. The ride turns right at the end on Route 56, but if you turn left and go ³/₁₀ mile you'll come to Hot Dog Annie's, a marvelously dilapidated, honky-tonk snack bar—1950s roadside kitsch at its best.

6. Turn right on Route 56 and go ⁷/₁₀ mile to end. The Leicester town green is on your left at the end.

7. Turn right at end and go 100 yards to stop sign (merge head-on into Route 9).

8. Follow directions for the long ride from number 16 to the end.

Auburn–Sutton–Oxford–
Charlton–Leicester

Number of miles: 31 (20 without Charlton–Leicester extension)
Terrain: Hilly.
Food: Grocery and restaurants in Oxford. Country store in Leicester.
Start: Auburn Plaza, Route 12, Auburn, just west of routes 290 and 395, and ½ mile northeast of Route 20. If you're coming from the east on Route 20, follow it to Prospect Street, at a traffic light 7/10 mile beyond Routes 395 and 290. Turn right on Prospect Street, and the shopping center is on your right.

This is a tour of rolling farm country, dotted with lakes, south and a little west of Worcester. Although close to the city, the region is delightfully rural because, unlike Boston and Springfield, Worcester has no dreary suburbs despoiling the surrounding area. Biking in this part of the state is challenging because the landscape is hilly, but you'll be rewarded with fine views from ridgetops, narrow lanes twisting past old barns and grazing cattle, and several stretches along ponds.

You start from Auburn, Worcester's closest approximation to a bedroom suburb, and immediately head into undeveloped countryside. You'll go along Ramshorn and Stockwell ponds and up and over ridges with fine views to Oxford, a pleasant community best known as the birthplace of Clara Barton, founder of the American Red Cross. From Oxford it's an easy run back to Auburn along a valley.

The long ride heads farther west into the rolling hills and ridges of Charlton and then Leicester (pronounced Lester). Just before the end is a delightful run along the Dark Brook Reservoir, bordered by a stately grove of pines.

Directions for the ride: 31 miles

1. Turn right out of parking lot onto Route 12 and go 2/10 mile to Faith

Avenue (unmarked) on right, at traffic light.

2. Turn right on Faith Avenue and go ½ mile to Route 20, at stop sign.

3. Cross Route 20 onto Oxford Street South. **CAUTION:** Watch for traffic. Go 1²/₁₀ miles to Cedar Street on left. You'll follow Eddy Pond on your left, on the far side of Route 395.

4. Turn left on Cedar Street and go ⁶/₁₀ mile to end (merge to right). There is no stop sign at the intersection.

5. Bear right at end, crossing railroad tracks, and go ²/₁₀ mile to end (Barnes Street on left, South Street on right).

6. Turn right at end onto South Street and go ⁶/₁₀ mile to Old Millbury Road on left, shortly after top of hill.

7. Turn left on Old Millbury Road (it's a fairly sharp left). Go 1⁸/₁₀ miles to Dolan Road on right. It comes up while you're going downhill. **CAUTION:** The first ½ mile is bumpy.

8. Turn right on Dolan Road and go ²/₁₀ mile to Davis Road on right.

9. Turn right on Davis Road and go 1⁸/₁₀ miles to end. You'll climb a tough hill and then descend steeply to the shore of Ramshorn Pond. **CAUTION:** Watch for bumps and sandy spots on the descent—take it easy.

10. Turn right at end onto Dolan Road and go ⁶/₁₀ mile to crossroads and stop sign at bottom of hill.

11. Turn right at stop sign and go 1²/₁₀ miles to Town Farm Road (unmarked), a small crossroads where the road on the right goes up a very steep hill. You'll follow three small ponds, the Stockwell Ponds, on your left.

12. Turn right at crossroads onto Town Farm Road up the hill—I won't blame you for walking it—and go 1¹/₁₀ miles to end. At the top of the hill you'll be rewarded by a panoramic view of rolling green hillsides. The hamlet of West Sutton is at the end.

13. Turn right at end onto Sutton and go 3⁶/₁₀ miles to traffic light (Route 12) in the center of Oxford. After a short climb, you'll relax on a gradual downhill run with fine views and pass Robinson Pond on the left. When you come to Route 12, notice the handsome red-brick town hall on the far side of the intersection. The short ride turns right on Route 12 and the long ride goes straight.

14. Cross Route 12 and go 2 miles to crossroads and stop sign (Conlin Road).

15. Go straight for 1⁴/₁₀ miles to end. You'll cross the Buffumville Reser-

voir, where there's a swimming area on your right, and cliumb a long, steady hill.

16. Turn right at end and go 1½ miles to Route 20, a four-lane highway, at stop sign and blinking light. There's a grocery on the far left corner.

17. Cross Route 20 diagonally (**CAUTION** here) and go ¹⁄₁₀ mile to fork (Hammond Hill Road, unmarked, bears left).

18. Bear left at fork onto Hammond Hill Road and go 1½ miles to end, at stop sign (merge to your right shortly after the bridge over the Massachusetts Turnpike).

19. Bear right at end and go ⁴⁄₁₀ mile to Smith Road, which bears left just after railroad bridge.

20. Bear left on Smith Road, go 100 yards to fork, and bear left again on main road. Go 2 miles to end. **CAUTION:** Watch for bumps and potholes for the first mile. At the end, a dam and millpond are on the far side of the intersection.

21. Turn right at end and go ¹⁄₁₀ mile to River Street (unmarked), which turns sharply left. A country store is at the intersection.

22. Turn sharply left onto River Street and go ³⁄₁₀ mile to Clark Street on right. You'll cross a tumbling brook and pass a fine white church on your left at the beginning.

23. Turn right on Clark Street and go ½ mile to crossroads and stop sign (Route 56).

24. Cross Route 56 and go ⁶⁄₁₀ mile to traffic island at bottom of hill, immediately after stop sign. Get into low gear at the intersection.

25. Turn sharply right onto Henshaw at traffic island up steep hill and go 1 mile to crossroads and stop sign.

26. Turn sharply left at crossroads onto Stafford (**CAUTION** here). Go 1½ miles to Auburn Street, a small diagonal crossroads where the road on the right turns sharply right. It comes up very suddenly while you're going downhill—don't whizz past it.

27. Turn sharply right on Auburn Street and go 1¹⁄₁₀ miles to end, at railroad bridge.

28. Turn left at end, going under railroad bridge. Immediately after the bridge, turn right on Leicester Street and go 1¹⁄₁₀ miles to crossroads and stop sign. You'll go along the Dark Brook Reservoir on your right.

29. Turn right at crossroads onto Warren, following the reservoir on your right, and go 1¹⁄₁₀ miles to end (Route 12).

30. Turn left on Route 12. Auburn Plaza is just ahead on right.

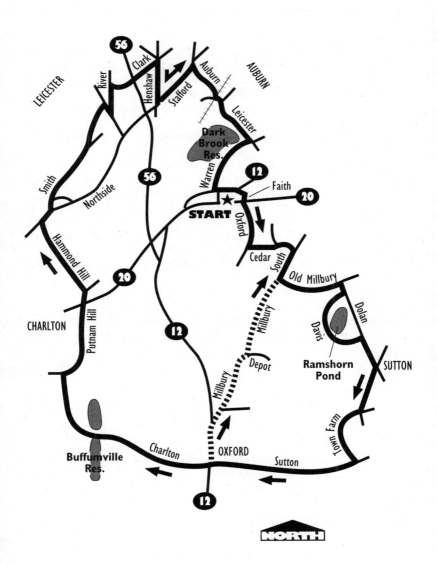

Directions for the ride: 20 miles

1. Follow the directions for the long ride through number 13.

2. Turn right on Route 12 and go $1\frac{1}{10}$ miles to Millbury Boulevard (unmarked), which bears right at a blinking light just after police station on right. Notice the attractive brick library on your left after $\frac{1}{10}$ mile. Then you'll pass the Oxford town green on your right.

3. Bear right on Millbury Boulevard and go $\frac{3}{10}$ mile to end (merge right at yield sign).

4. Bear right and go 100 yards to Millbury Road on left, immediately after railroad tracks.

5. Turn left on Millbury Road and go $\frac{9}{10}$ mile to fork immediately after the Route 395 access road on left. **CAUTION:** There are diagonal railroad tracks on this section, and there's another set of tracks at the fork.

6. Bear left at fork onto Millbury Road. After $1\frac{1}{10}$ miles Old Millbury Road bears right, but bear slightly left on the main road. Go $\frac{6}{10}$ mile to your first left, South Street (unmarked). **CAUTION:** Watch for bumps and cracks.

7. Turn left on South Street and go $\frac{2}{10}$ mile to fork immediately after railroad tracks (Cedar Street bears left).

8. Bear left on Cedar Street and go $\frac{6}{10}$ mile to end, at stop sign.

9. Turn right at end and go $1\frac{2}{10}$ miles to Route 20, at stop sign.

10. Turn left on Route 20. (**CAUTION:** Busy intersection.) Go $\frac{1}{2}$ mile to Prospect Street, at traffic light. The shopping center is just ahead on your right.

Old Sturbridge Village Ride:
Sturbridge–Brimfield–Warren–Brookfield

Number of miles: 32 (15 without Brimfield–Warren extension)
Terrain: The short ride is rolling, with one long, steady hill. The long ride is hilly.
Road surface: 100 yards of dirt road.
Food: Grocery and snack bar in Brimfield and Warren. Burger King at end.
Start: Burger King, Route 20, Sturbridge, just east of Old Sturbridge Village.

The magnificent ridge, valley, and lake country of south-central Massachusetts provides superb bicycling on a network of nearly untraveled country roads, with spectacular vistas spread before you as you crest each ridge. The ride passes through Brimfield and Warren, two of the numerous classic New England towns dotting the middle of the state.

The ride starts across the road from Old Sturbridge Village, an outstanding historical restoration, among the best in the country. If you've never been there, it would be worthwhile to set aside several hours before or after the ride to visit it. With painstaking historical research and attention to detail, Old Sturbridge Village re-creates life in a early nineteenth-century New England community as closely as possible. No power mowers trim the green—sheep do the job just as effectively. Dirt paths become muddy when it rains and dusty in the summer heat just as in 1800, when the luxury of blacktop hadn't diffused to the country towns. In the ramshackle little shops and outbuildings, apprentices dressed in historically accurate garments learn and apply traditional unmechanized crafts and trades like spinning yarn, making watertight casks, tanning leather, blacksmithing, and cabinetmaking. No attempt has been made to artificially glamorize the village or dress it up. As in most post-Revolutionary small towns, it has only one impressive house, which belonged to the community's most prominent family; everyone

Spring plowing at Old Sturbridge Village

else lived in simple, sparsely furnished cottages, scratching a living from the soil, a small business, or a trade.

Old Sturbridge Village also has several galleries exhibiting artifacts from everyday life in early New England, a fascinating garden of medicinal and culinary herbs, and a full range of educational programs.

The success of Old Sturbridge Village has spawned several other attractions, including a doll museum, an antique auto museum, Saint Anne's Shrine with a collection of Russian icons, and too many overpriced antiques and crafts shops.

From Sturbridge you'll head into lake country, going along the Brimfield Reservoir. Just off the route is East Brimfield Dam, holding the waters in place. A couple of miles ahead you'll pass beautiful Holland Pond, where you can take a swim. Next you go through a valley to the elegant old town of Brimfield. The larger-than-average green is framed by a graceful white church, rambling old wooden homes, and an ornate pink-purple Victorian town hall. From Brimfield you'll head north past Sherman Pond into inspiring ridge-and-valley country. It's a long climb to the top of the ridge, but you'll be rewarded by sweeping views of the rolling, open countryside.

The route continues farther north into more rural, equally spectacular ridge-and-valley country. You'll enjoy a long descent into Warren, an unspoiled jewel of a small town built around a central square. Framing the square are the brick town hall adorned with a bell tower, an old-fashioned former train station (now used for offices), the handsome stone library, the town green with a bandstand on it, and a white church on top of the hill.

There's a long, tough climb out of Warren. After a couple of miles you'll cross the town line into Brookfield. Here you'll bike past gracious horse farms, with views of Quaboag Pond and distant hills in the background, and then hug the shore of Quacumquasit Pond. The return to Sturbridge leads through woods and small farms along a quiet country road.

The short ride heads directly toward Brookfield on a quiet back road, bypassing Holland Pond and Brimfield.

Directions for the ride: 32 miles ༺༅༅༅༅༅

1. Turn right (west) out of parking lot onto Route 20 and go almost $\frac{9}{10}$

mile to Arnold Road on right. It's immediately after an attractive red-brick building (currently a senior citizens' center) on the right. Here the short ride turns right and the long ride goes straight.

2. Continue straight on Route 20 for 2²/₁₀ miles to Holland–East Brimfield Road on your left, at the far end of the Brimfield Reservoir (sign may say TO QUINEBAUG COVE CAMPGROUND). After ¹/₂ mile you'll see the Victorian building in the center of Fiskdale on your right, newly renovated into shops and offices. Just after the building, Saint Anne's Shrine is on your right up a short hill. To visit East Brimfield Dam, turn left ⁶/₁₀ mile beyond Route 148 on Riverview Avenue, opposite a motel. The dam is ¹/₄ mile ahead.

3. Turn left on Holland–East Brimfield Road and go 1⁹/₁₀ miles to Morse Road, which turns right downhill. It's just after Long Hill Road turns left up a steep hill.

4. Turn right on Morse Road and go ¹/₄ mile to Morse lane, a dirt road that turns sharply left. There's a red, barn-shaped building on the left at the intersection.

5. Turn sharply left on Morse Lane (don't turn 90 degrees left onto dirt driveway). Go 100 yards to crossroads at bottom of hill. Holland Pond is in front of you at the intersection. **CAUTION:** The dirt road is rough and rocky, and the crossroads is sandy. It's safest to walk.

6. Turn right at bottom of hill onto paved road, following pond on left. Go ¹/₂ mile to end (Holland Road). **CAUTION:** Watch for potholes.

7. Turn right at end onto Holland and go 3¹/₁₀ miles to end, at stop sign (merge left on Route 20).

8. Bear left on Route 20 (**CAUTION** here). Go ⁴/₁₀ mile to Brookfield Road on right, at a traffic island with a monument in the middle. Just before the intersection, notice the old wooden windmill on your left. At the monument the ride turns right, but it's worth going straight for ²/₁₀ mile to see the lovely Brimfield town green and the unique Victorian town hall. There's also a grocery and snack bar opposite the green.

9. Turn right on Brookfield Road and go 4⁴/₁₀ miles to fork where Brookfield Road bears right and Southbridge Road (unmarked) bears left. It's just after Southbridge Road Extension on right. You'll pass Sherman Pond and then make the long ascent to the top of the ridge.

10. Bear left on Southbridge Road and go 3⁷/₁₀ miles to another fork, where Washington Road bears right and the main road bears slightly left downhill. It comes up at the bottom of a long downhill run. After a

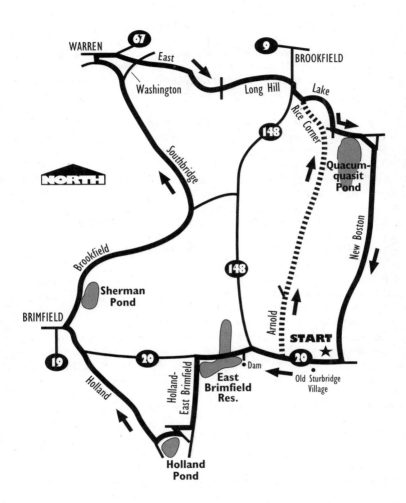

WARREN

67

East

Washington

9

BROOKFIELD

Long Hill

Lake

Rice Corner

148

Quacum-
quasit
Pond

Southbridge

NORTH

New Boston

Brookfield

148

**Sherman
Pond**

BRIMFIELD

Arnold

START

19

20

20

Holland

Holland-
East Brimfield

**East
Brimfield
Res.**

Dam

Old Sturbridge
Village

**Holland
Pond**

tough climb at the beginning, this is a magnificent run along ridges with panoramic views.

11. Bear left downhill at fork (still Southbridge Road). Go ½ mile to a road on the right that goes under a railroad bridge. It's at the bottom of the hill.

12. Turn right under railroad bridge and go 100 yards to a small traffic circle with a monument on it. This is the center of Warren. The yellow-brick town hall is to your left, the old railroad depot and town green are on your right, and the elegant stone library is in front of you a little to the right.

13. Turn right at traffic circle on Route 67, passing the library on your left. Go ²⁄₁₀ mile to East Road, which bears right uphill.

14. Bear right on East Road and go ³⁄₁₀ mile to diagonal crossroads at top of hill. This is a steep climb.

15. Continue straight uphill on East Road and go 2½ miles to crossroads and stop sign. **CAUTION:** It comes up while you're going downhill. This stretch has some steep ups and downs; take it easy on the descents.

16. Continue straight for 2½ miles to end (Route 148). **CAUTION:** Steep descent at the beginning.

17. Turn right on Route 148 and go 100 yards to Lake Road, which bears left.

18. Bear left on Lake Road and go ¼ mile to fork where Rice Corner Road goes straight and Lake Road bears left.

19. Bear left again on Lake Road and go 2¹⁄₁₀ miles to end. (The end is almost a crossroads—Allen Road, unmarked, is on the far side of the intersection about 20 feet to your right.) This is an inspiring run along a hillside past estates and horse farms, with views of Quaboag Pond below.

20. Turn left at end and go ⁷⁄₁₀ mile to fork. In the middle of the fork is a large traffic island with trees on it. You'll pass Quacumquasit Pond on your right.

21. Bear right at fork onto New Boston and go 4⁸⁄₁₀ miles to end (Route 20).

22. Turn right on Route 20 and go almost ⁴⁄₁₀ mile to Burger King on right.

Directions for the ride: 15 miles 〰〰〰〰

1. Turn right (west) out of parking lot onto Route 20. Go almost ⁹⁄₁₀ mile

to Arnold Road on right. It's immediately after an attractive red-brick building (currently a senior citizens' center) on the right.

2. Turn right on Arnold Road and go 1^7/$_{10}$ miles to fork (Lake Road, a smaller road, bears left).

3. Curve slightly right on the main road and go 3^3/$_{10}$ miles to end (merge left at stop sign on Rice Corner Road).

4. Bear left on Rice Corner Road and go 1^4/$_{10}$ miles to Lake Road on right.

5. Turn right on Lake Road and go 2^1/$_{10}$ miles to end. (The end is almost a crossroads—Allen Road, unmarked, is on the far side of the intersection about 20 feet to your right.) This is an inspiring run along a hillside past estates and horse farms, with views of Quaboag Pond below.

6. Follow the directions for the long ride from number 20 to the end.

Bowen House, Woodstock

Southbridge–
Woodstock, Connecticut

Number of miles: 24 (14 without Woodstock extension)
Terrain: Very rolling, with several short, steep hills.
Food: Country store in Woodstock. McDonald's at end.
Start: Shopping center behind McDonald's, Route 131, Southbridge, 1½ miles east of the center of town.

This ride has us explore the very rural, very rolling, ridge-and-valley country straddling the Massachusetts-Connecticut border roughly midway between Worcester and Springfield. Steep-sided wooded ridges, running north to south, become more open and rounded as you head south into Connecticut. The long ride passes through the magnificent hilltop town of Woodstock, Connecticut.

You start from the small industrial city of Southbridge, one of the most attractive mill towns in Massachusetts. Southbridge is a one-industry town—optical products—with factories of the largest company, American Optical, lining the banks of the Quinebaug River in a seemingly endless row. The company's main building is a massive yet graceful Victorian structure resembling an Elizabethan castle. American Optical was founded in 1833, making the city the first producer of optical goods in the country. In the downtown area, graceful Victorian buildings of brick line the wide, gently curving main street, which leads up a hill to a large, graceful church standing proudly over the town.

From Southbridge you'll head south through open farmland and along unspoiled Morse Pond into Connecticut. After a few miles on country lanes winding past old farms and broad fields, you cross back into Massachusetts and follow the crest of a high ridge with spectacular views. The descent back into Southbridge is a screamer.

The long ride heads farther south into Connecticut to the unspoiled hilltop town of Woodstock, a classic New England jewel. Framing the large green are the traditional white church, the handsome old wooden main building of Woodstock Academy, and the Bowen House, a marvelous pink Gothic mansion. Also called Roseland Cottage, it was built in 1846 by Henry C. Bowen, a businessman who invited presidents Grant, Hayes, Harrison, and McKinley there for Fourth of July gatherings. Now run by the Society for the Preservation of New England Antiquities and open to the public afternoons from May to October, the mansion has period furnishings and a private bowling alley, one of the earliest in the country.

Beyond Woodstock you'll weave through inspiring, very rolling farmland and rejoin the short ride just in time to enjoy the high ridge and fast descent into Southbridge.

Directions for the ride: 24 miles 〰️〰️〰️〰️

1. Turn left out of parking lot onto Route 131 and go ¼ mile to Ashland Avenue on right. Route 131 curves sharply left at the intersection.
2. Turn right on Ashland Avenue and go $3/10$ mile to crossroads and stop sign (Route 169). There's a short, steep hill at the beginning.
3. Turn left on Route 169. After $28/10$ miles you'll enter Connecticut. Continue $24/10$ miles to English Neighborhood Road, which turns sharply right almost at the bottom of hill just before a blinking light (Route 197). Here the short ride makes a sharp right and the long ride goes straight.
4. Go straight on Route 169 for $1/10$ mile to Route 197, at stop sign and blinking light. This is the hamlet of North Woodstock. Notice the graceful white church on the far left corner.
5. Continue straight for $32/10$ miles to the pink Bowen House on your right, opposite the Woodstock town green. The main building of Woodstock Academy, with an ornate belfry, is opposite the Bowen House on your left, at the top of the grassy hill.
6. From the Bowen House, continue on Route 169 for $4/10$ mile to Plaine Hill Road (unmarked), which bears slightly right where Route 169 curves left downhill. There's a magnificent view to the left at the intersection.
7. Bear slightly right on Plaine Hill Road and go ½ mile to end (Route 171), at bottom of steep hill. **CAUTION** here.
8. Turn right on Route 171 and go $27/10$ miles to crossroads (Shields Road on left, Coatney Hill Road on right).
9. Turn right on Coatney Hill Road and go $12/10$ miles to crossroads and stop sign.

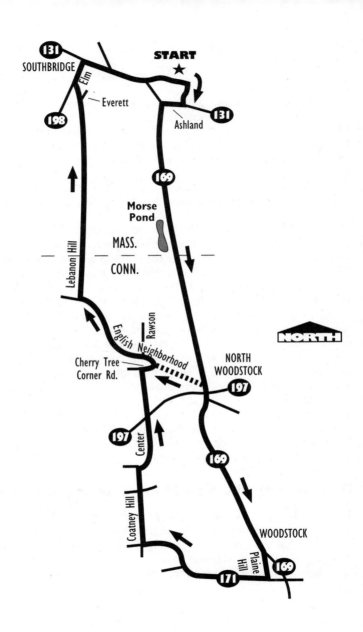

10. Continue straight onto Center School Road. Go $^3/_{10}$ mile to end (Center Road, unmarked).

11. Turn right on Center Road and go $1^1/_{10}$ miles to diagonal crossroads and stop sign (Route 197).

12. Cross Route 197 and go $^9/_{10}$ mile to fork where the main road (Cherry Tree Corner Road) bears right.

13. Bear right on Cherry Tree Corner Road and go $^1/_{10}$ mile to end.

14. Turn left at end onto English Neighborhood. Go $^3/_{10}$ mile to fork where Rawson Road bears right and the main road bears slightly left downhill.

15. Bear left on main road (English Neighborhood) and go $1^1/_2$ miles to Lebanon Hill Road on right, immediately after brick ranch house on right.

16. Turn right on Lebanon Hill Road. Go $3^8/_{10}$ miles to fork where Everett Street bears right and the main road (Elm Street, unmarked) bears slightly left. It's just after you enter the built-up section of Southbridge. After $^9/_{10}$ mile of riding on Lebanon Hill Road, at the Massachusetts line, there's a granite marker dated 1906. The wooden chapel was built in 1995. Then you'll have a thrilling downhill run with magnificent views.

17. Bear slightly left on Elm Street and go $^1/_2$ mile to end (Route 131), in downtown Southbridge. Just before the end, notice the castlelike town hall on the right, built in 1888, and the clock-towered fire station on the left. When you come to Route 131, the main business district is on your left.

18. Turn right on Route 131 and go $^4/_{10}$ mile to rotary. At the rotary, glance to your left and see the castlelike main building of American Optical Company.

19. Bear right at rotary onto Routes 131 and 169. Go $^6/_{10}$ mile to fork, where Route 131 goes straight and Route 169 bears right uphill. You'll follow the Quinebaug River on your left.

20. Go straight on Route 131 for $^4/_{10}$ mile to McDonald's on left.

Directions for the ride: 14 miles

1. Follow directions for the long ride through number 3.

2. Turn sharply right on English Neighborhood Road. Go $1^4/_{10}$ miles to fork where Rawson Road bears right and the main road bears slightly left downhill. Most of this section is uphill.

3. Follow directions for the long ride from number 15 to the end.

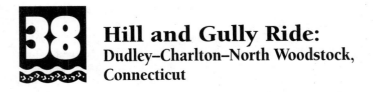

Hill and Gully Ride:
Dudley–Charlton–North Woodstock, Connecticut

Number of miles: 31 (22 with shortcut omitting North Woodstock)
Terrain: Hilly.
Food: Grocery and snack bar in Charlton. Restaurant in Quinebaug.
Start: Dudley Plaza, a shopping center on Airport Road, Dudley. It's just north of Route 197, 2 miles west of downtown Webster. An alternate starting point, closer to the Worcester area, is the small shopping center on Route 31 in Charlton, 1 mile south of Route 20. Directions for the Charlton start are at the end. The Dudley start offers the advantage that most of the second half of the ride is downhill.

The rolling, rural countryside between Worcester and Springfield consists primarily of high, open ridges that provide some of the most spectacular bicycle riding in the state. This ride tours the southeastern portion of the region, ascending and descending from one ridge to another on smooth, lightly traveled roads with sweeping vistas around every bend. The graceful New England hilltop towns of Charlton and Dudley add to the appeal and variety of the ride.

The ride starts from Dudley, a two-faced town with old, grim mills on the Quinebaug River that forms the border with Webster, and with a classic town center 3 miles to the west, surrounded by broad expanses of farmland. You'll go past the massive granite Stevens Mill, built in 1864, and ride alongside Pierpont Meadow Pond, framed by rustic houses and cottages nestled in the woods. The route proceeds into the ridge country to Charlton, among the most appealing and spectacularly located central Massachusetts towns. The handsome church, turn-of-the-century brick schoolhouse, town hall, and an old cemetery crown the top of a hill with superb views to the west. From here you'll head south to Dudley on Route 31, an absolute paradise for biking. Three miles out of town is the Dresser Hill Dairy, with some of the best ice cream in Worcester County. From here you'll climb onto more open ridges with inspiring vistas, dip downhill, climb and dip some more, and finally enjoy a thrilling 2-mile descent into the Quinebaug Valley.

The route continues south through more glorious ridge-and-valley country to the pristine hamlet of North Woodstock, Connecticut, which contains only a graceful white church and a few sturdy, well-kept houses. Near the end of the ride you'll climb one more hill to the gracious town center of Dudley. It consists primarily of Nichols College, which is mainly a business school. Adjoining the campus are some handsome old homes and a distinctive brick church with a tall, slender clock tower. From here it's a short downhill ride to the end.

Directions for the rides: Dudley start

1. Turn left out of parking lot onto Airport Road (don't get on Alton Drive Extension), and immediately turn left onto Route 197. Go $1^1/_{10}$ miles to traffic light where Route 12 (Schofield Avenue) turns right and Village Street turns left.

2. Turn left on Village Street and go $^3/_{10}$ mile to Charlton Road (unmarked), which bears left at a small traffic island. You'll pass underneath a section of the massive Stevens Mill, built in 1864.

3. Bear left on Charlton Road and go $1^6/_{10}$ miles to Pierpont Road on left, shortly after a large grassy traffic island with a monument on it.

4. Turn left on Pierpont Road and go $1^9/_{10}$ miles to crossroads and stop sign (Potter Village Road). You'll follow Pierpont Meadow Pond on your right.

5. Go straight for $^7/_{10}$ mile to the top of a hill where the main road turns 90 degrees right and another road turns left. The Granite Reservoir is in front of you at the intersection, set back a short distance from the road.

6. Curve sharply right on main road, following the Granite Reservoir on your left. Go $^6/_{10}$ mile to crossroads and stop sign (Colburn Road on left, A.F. Putnam Road on right).

7. Go straight for $1^4/_{10}$ miles to end (Oxford Road).

8. Turn left at end and go $^1/_2$ mile to Morton Station Road on right. It comes up as you start to go downhill—don't whizz past it.

9. Turn right on Morton Station Road and go $^1/_2$ mile to end.

10. Turn left at end and go $1^1/_2$ miles to crossroads and stop sign (Route 31). You'll pass an orchard on your right as soon as you turn left. When

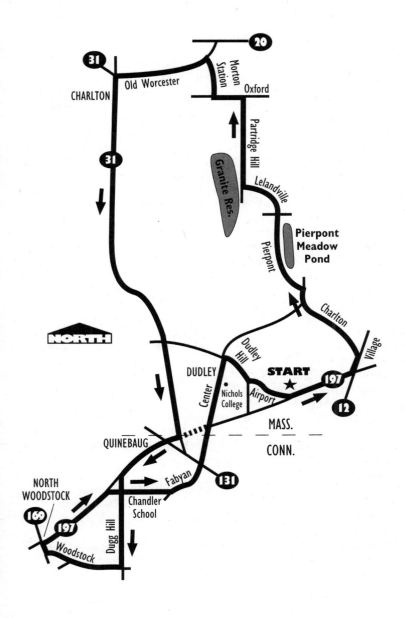

you get to Route 31, a grocery and snack bar are on the far side of the intersection.

11. Turn left (south) on Route 31 and go 8¹⁄₁₀ miles to crossroads and blinking light at bottom of long hill (Route 197). At the beginning of this stretch you'll go through the center of Charlton. The Dresser Hill Dairy is 3 miles ahead on your right, atop a ridge. Immediately after the dairy, go straight (don't bear right downhill). **CAUTION** on the descents—keep alert for bumps and cracks.

When you get to Route 197, the ride turns right, but you can shorten the distance to 22 miles by turning left. Go ½ mile to unmarked crossroads where a sign may point left TO NICHOLS COLLEGE (Fabyan Road on right, Center Road on left). Turn left and go 1⁴⁄₁₀ miles to crossroads and stop sign (Dudley Hill Road), shortly after Nichols College and brick church on left. It's a tough climb to the college. Resume with direction number 23.

12. Turn right on Route 197 and go ²⁄₁₀ mile to traffic light (Route 131). This is the village of Quinebaug, Connecticut, which is 200 yards south of the Massachusetts border.

13. Continue on Route 197 for 1⁴⁄₁₀ miles to diagonal crossroads, where Converse Road turns sharply right and Dugg Hill Road bears left.

14. Bear left on Dugg Hill Road. Just ahead is a crossroads and stop sign (Chandler School Road). Continue straight for 1⁷⁄₁₀ miles to another crossroads and stop sign at bottom of hill (Hibbard Road on left, Woodstock Road on right).

15. Turn right at bottom of hill. Go 1²⁄₁₀ miles to fork where County Road bears left and the main road curves right. You'll go through the hamlet of East Woodstock, Connecticut.

16. Curve right on main road and go ½ mile to end (Route 169).

17. Turn right on Route 169 and go ¹⁄₁₀ mile to Route 197, at stop sign and blinking light. This is North Woodstock, another tiny village.

18. Turn right on Route 197 and go 1⁸⁄₁₀ miles to Chandler School Road, which bears right.

19. Bear right on Chandler School Road. Just ahead is a crossroads and stop sign (Dugg Hill Road). Continue straight for 1¹⁄₁₀ miles to end (merge left at stop sign). **CAUTION:** You reach the end suddenly at bottom of short hill.

20. Bear left at end onto Fabyan and go ⁹⁄₁₀ mile to stop sign and blinking light (Route 131). There's a grocery on the far left corner.

21. Cross Route 131 and go $^7/_{10}$ mile to crossroads and stop sign (Route 197). **CAUTION:** Diagonal railroad tracks at the beginning.

22. Cross Route 197 and go $1^4/_{10}$ miles to crossroads and stop sign (Dudley Hill Road) shortly after Nichols College and brick church on left. It's a tough climb to the college.

23. Turn right at crossroads. Go $^4/_{10}$ mile to fork where Dudley Hill Road bears right and Airport Road bears left.

24. Bear left on Airport Road and go $^6/_{10}$ mile to shopping center on left, at bottom of hill.

Directions for the rides: Charlton Start 〰️〰️〰️
(Start at the small shopping center on Route 31.)

1. Turn right (south) onto Route 31 and go $8^1/_{10}$ miles to crossroads and blinking light at bottom of long hill (Route 197). After 3 miles you'll pass the Dresser Hill Dairy on your right, atop a ridge. Immediately after the dairy, go straight (don't bear right downhill). **CAUTION** on the descents—keep alert for bumps and cracks.

When you get to Route 197, the ride turns right, but you can shorten the distance to 22 miles by turning left. See direction number 11 for the ride starting in Dudley.

2. Follow directions number 12 through 24, and then 1 through 10, for the ride starting in Dudley.

Tri-State Tour:
Webster–Douglas–Pascoag, Rhode Island–Thompson, Connecticut

Number of miles: 33 (19 without Pascoag–Thompson extension)
Terrain: Rolling, with one tough hill.
Food: Groceries at two campgrounds in Sutton, open during camping season. Grocery and snack bar in Pascoag. Friendly Ice Cream at end.
Start: Friendly Ice Cream, Route 12, Webster, just west of Route 395.

This is a tour of the very rural, mostly wooded, lake-studded countryside surrounding the point where Massachusetts, Rhode Island, and Connecticut meet. The terrain is not as hilly as in the surrounding areas. The lightly traveled back roads, winding through the woods and along several ponds, promise enjoyable and peaceful bicycling.

The ride starts in Webster, a small and rather bleak mill city on the French River just north of the Connecticut line. You'll immediately head into rolling, wooded countryside to the tiny village of West Sutton and pass Sutton Falls, a small dam with a little covered bridge above it. Just ahead are pleasant runs along Manchaug Pond and then Whitins Reservoir, where you'll pass a waterslide (here's your chance to descend a different type of hill). From here it's a short way to the graceful, classic New England village of Douglas, with a stately white church, old cemetery, and triangular green.

From Douglas you'll follow a smooth secondary road to the attractive little mill town of Pascoag, in the northwestern corner of Rhode Island. With massive granite and brick Victorian mills straight out of the Industrial Revolution, Pascoag is typical of the many mill villages hugging the fast-flowing rivers throughout Rhode Island. Leaving Pascoag, you'll skirt the Wilson Reservoir and then climb gradually to the top of Buck Hill, one of Rhode Island's highest points.

You now speed down two steep hills into the northeastern corner of Connecticut. After about three miles of narrow lanes, you'll cross back into Webster and return into town along the shore of Lake Chargoggagoggmanchaugagoggchaubunagungamaug (usually called Webster

Lake), which in the Nipmuc Indian language means, "I fish on my side, you fish on your side, and nobody fishes in the middle." If it hasn't been stolen, a sign spelling out the name of the lake may greet you as you cross the state line.

The short ride heads directly from Douglas back to Webster without leaving Massachusetts. There's a great downhill run at the end, and you'll ride along Webster Lake at the bottom.

Directions for the ride: 33 miles

1. Turn left (east) out of parking lot. Just ahead, go straight at traffic light onto Route 16 East. Go $3/10$ mile to Sutton Road on left, immediately after the Route 395 underpass.

2. Turn left on Sutton Road (**CAUTION** here). Go $3/10$ mile to where Sutton Road turns right and Cudworth Road goes straight.

3. Turn right (still Sutton Road) and go $3\,8/10$ miles to end. You'll pass Nipmuck Pond on your right.

4. Turn right at end. After $2/10$ mile, Douglas Road bears right uphill, but bear slightly left downhill, staying on the main road. Go 1 mile to Manchaug Road on right (it's unmarked; a sign may say SUTTON FALLS CAMPING AREA). It's your second right, and it comes up almost at the bottom of a long descent. You'll ride through the hamlet of West Sutton.

5. Turn right on Manchaug Road. After $8/10$ mile, watch for the Sutton Falls Camping Area on your right, with its fine little dam and covered bridge. A small grocery store here is open during camping season. You'll see Manchaug Pond on your right.

6. From the campground, continue $1\frac{1}{2}$ miles to a fork where one road bears left and Torrey Road continues straight down a steep hill. You'll follow Manchaug Pond on your right.

7. Go straight down the hill for $3/10$ mile to Holt Road, which bears right at pond.

8. Bear right on Holt Road. Go $1\,3/10$ miles to fork where Wallis Street bears right and Northwest Main Street bears left, immediately after stop sign. You'll pass another grocery on the right near the beginning.

9. Bear left on Northwest Main Street and go $7/10$ mile to another fork. You'll follow Whitins Reservoir on your right and pass a waterslide after $2/10$ mile.

10. Bear right at fork, following the water on your right, and go $8/10$ mile

to end (merge left on Wallis Street). There is no stop sign here. **CAUTION:** Watch for bumps and sand at the begininng.

11. Bear left at end and go ⁶/₁₀ mile to fork.

12. Bear left at fork and go ⁴/₁₀ mile to another fork at church on right. This is Douglas.

13. Bear right at fork and go ¹/₁₀ mile to end (merge right onto Route 16). Immediately ahead is a blinking light where Route 16 (Webster Street) turns right. Here the short ride turns right onto Route 16 and the long ride goes straight.

14. Go straight where Route 16 turns right. Immediately ahead is a fork, where Route 96 bears left.

15. Bear left on Route 96 and go 6⁶/₁₀ miles to end (school Street on left, Hill Road on right). Route 96 turns left here. The second half of this long stretch is in Rhode Island.

16. Turn left at end (still Route 96) and go ¹/₁₀ mile to River Street on right, immediately after a small bridge. A sign may say TO ROUTE 107.

17. Turn right on River Street and go ¹/₁₀ mile to end (Route 107, Chapel Street).

18. Bear right on Route 107 and go 1⁴/₁₀ miles to end, opposite a super-market in the center of Pascoag, Rhode Island. Route 107 twists and turns, but stay on the main road. Just before the end you'll cross a stream with a small waterfall on your left.

19. Turn left at end, in front of supermarket (still Route 107), and go 1 block to end (Route 100 on right).

20. Turn right on Route 100. After 100 yards Route 100 turns 90 degrees right. Continue on Route 100 for 3²/₁₀ miles to Buck Hill Road, a smaller road that bears left (signs may say TO CONNECTICUT ROUTE 12 and TO BUCK HILL CAMPGROUND). About 1 mile out of Pascoag you'll pass a wonderful old red country schoolhouse on your right. Then you'll go by the Wilson Reservoir.

21. Bear left on Buck Hill Road and go ¹/₁₀ mile to fork where the main road bears left.

22. Bear left at fork and go 3 miles to end (merge to right at bottom of second long descent, at yield sign). You are now in Connecticut. **CAU-TION:** Watch for sand at the end.

23. Bear right at bottom of second hill. This is Quaddick Town Farm Road (unmarked). Stay on the main road for 1²/₁₀ miles to end. Notice the old church, built in 1841, at the intersection.

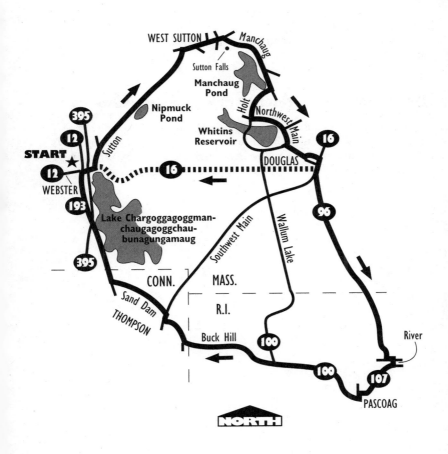

WEST SUTTON   Manchaug

Sutton Falls

Manchaug Pond

Nipmuck Pond

Holt

Northwest Main

Whitins Reservoir

395

12

START ★

12

WEBSTER

Sutton

16

DOUGLAS

16

193

**Lake Chargoggagoggman-
chaugagoggchau-
bunagungamaug**

Southwest Main

Wallum Lake

96

395

CONN.

MASS.

R.I.

Sand Dam

THOMPSON

Buck Hill

100

100

River

100

107

PASCOAG

NORTH

24. Turn right at end and go $\frac{1}{10}$ mile to fork (East Thompson Road bears right; Sand Dam Road bears left).

25. Bear left on Sand Dam Road and go 2 miles to end, at stop sign (merge right on Route 193).

26. Bear right on Route 193 and go 3 miles to the third traffic light (Routes 16 and 12). You'll pass Webster Lake on the right.

27. Turn left on Route 12 (**CAUTION:** Busy intersection). Friendly's is just ahead on right.

Directions for the ride: 19 miles

1. Follow directions for the long ride through number 13.

2. Turn right at blinking light on Route 16 and go 7 miles to Friendly's on right. It's just past the traffic light after the Route 395 underpass. You'll have a great downhill run coming into Webster, and pass Webster lake on your left.

Appendix

Bicycle Clubs

If you would like to bike with a group and meet other people who enjoy cycling, join a bicycle club. Most clubs have weekend rides of comfortable length, with a shortcut if you don't want to go too far. Usually a club will provide maps and mark the route by painting arrows in the road so that nobody gets lost. Joining a club is especially valuable if you don't have a car, because you'll meet people who do and who'll be able to give you a lift to areas beyond biking distance from home. To find out about clubs in your area, ask at any good bike shop. Addresses of clubs riding in western and central Massachusetts (subject to change) are as follows:

Bicycle Coalition of Massachusetts, 214A Broadway, Cambridge, MA 02139 (phone 617–491–RIDE). A political action group devoted to improving conditions for bicyclists. It has recently expanded its coverage from Greater Boston to the entire state.

Seven Hills Wheelmen, Box 24, Greendale Station, Worcester, MA 01606.

Fitchburg Cycling Club, Box 411, Lunenburg, MA 01462.

Cyclonauts Bicycling Club, 34 Call Street, Chicopee, MA 01013. Springfield area.

Franklin–Hampshire Freewheelers, 14 Lawndale Street, Easthampton, MA 01027.

Berkshire Velo Club, c/o The Arcadian Shop, 333 Pittsfield–Lenox Road (Routes 7 and 20), Lenox, MA 01240. More racing-oriented than recreational, but they may have some relaxed rides.

Northeast Sport Cyclists, 55 Franklin Avenue, Westfield, MA 01085.

Most of these clubs are affiliated with the League of American Bicyclists, which is the main national organization of and for bicyclists. It publishes an excellent monthly magazine and has a dynamic legislative-action program. The address of the league is 190 West Ostend Street, Suite 120, Baltimore, MD 21230-3755.

There are certainly other clubs in the state that I'm not aware of. Your local bike shop will know about them.

Further Reading and Resources

Massachusetts is covered by other bicycling guides if you'd like to explore new territory:

Short Bike Rides in Eastern Massachusetts, Second Edition, by Howard Stone. Old Saybrook, CT: Globe Pequot Press, 1997.
Short Bike Rides on Cape Cod, Nantucket and the Vineyard, Fifth Edition, by Jane Griffith and Edwin Mullen. Old Saybrook, CT: Globe Pequot Press, 1994.
Bicycle Touring in the Pioneer Valley, Revised and Expanded Edition, by Nancy Jane. Amherst: University of Massachusetts Press, 1996.
The Best Bike Rides in New England, Third Edition, by Paul D. Thomas. Old Saybrook, CT: Globe Pequot Press, 1996.
The Bicyclist's Guide to the Southern Berkshires, by Steve Lyons. Lenox, MA: Freewheel Publications, 1993.
Bike Rides in the Berkshire Hills, Revised and Updated Edition, by Lewis C. Cuyler. Stockbridge, MA: Berkshire House, 1995.
New England Over the Handlebars, by Michael Farny. Boston: Little, Brown, 1975.

A bicycling map of western and central Massachusetts is currently being prepared by BikeMaps Massachusetts; publication is planned for 1997.

About the Author

Howard Stone grew up in Boston, went to college in Maine and Illinois, and returned to his native New England, where he is now a librarian at Brown University. For many years Howard was the touring director of the Narragansett Bay Wheelmen, the major bicycle club for southeastern Massachusetts and Rhode Island. He is the author of *Short Bike Rides in Eastern Massachusetts* and *Short Bike Rides in Rhode Island,* also published by The Globe Pequot Press, and two other bicycling guides. Howard has done extensive bicycle touring, including a cross-country trip from Newport, Oregon, to Newport, Rhode Island, in 1978.